DEPRESSION AND HOPE

Books by Howard W. Stone

How to Think Theologically
(with James O. Duke, 1996)

Theological Context for Pastoral Caregiving:
Word in Deed
(1996)

Brief Pastoral Counseling:
Short-Term Approaches and Strategies
(1994)

Crisis Counseling
(Creative Pastoral Care and Counseling series, 1993)

The Caring Church:
A Guide for Lay Pastoral Care
(1991)

Handbook for Basic Types of Pastoral Care and Counseling
(with William Clements, 1991)

Christian Caring: Schleiermacher's Practical Theology
(with James O. Duke, 1988)

Using Behavioral Methods in Pastoral Counseling
(1980)

Suicide and Grief
(1972)

DEPRESSION AND HOPE

NEW INSIGHTS FOR PASTORAL COUNSELING

Howard W. Stone

FORTRESS PRESS

Minneapolis

Cover design: Brad Norr
Interior design: Julie Odland Smith

Library of Congress Cataloging-in-Publication Data
Stone, Howard W.
    Depression and hope : new insights for pastoral counseling / Howard W. Stone.
        p.   cm.
    Includes bibliographical references.
    ISBN 0-8006-3139-0 (alk. paper)
    1. Depressed persons—Pastoral counseling of.   2. Depression, Mental—Religious aspects—Christianity.   I. Title.
    BV4461.S76   1998
    259'.425—dc21   98–17840
                                                                                        CIP

The paper used in this publication meets the minimum requirements of American National Standard for Information Sciences—Permanence of Paper for Printed Library Materials, ANSI Z329.48-1984.   ∞™

Manufactured in the U.S.A.   AF 1-3139

02   01   00   99   98   1   2   3   4   5   6   7   8   9   10

To Karen Stone

Contents

Prologue

This year alone, one out of ten adults in the United States will feel the hopelessness, isolation, and inner barrenness of depression. The incidence of this affliction, which saps our energy and spirit, is increasing steadily and has been for the last half century.

If you sit in a worship service with roughly one hundred other people, chances are good that about ten of them will suffer from melancholia at some point during the year. There may be more. Perhaps you are one of them. With an average 10% of their congregations suffering from depression each year, clergy inevitably offer care and counseling for it.

In a recent study (Benner 1992), parish pastors were asked to list the five concerns that they most often faced with parishioners. Sixty-four percent of them identified depression, topped only by marriage and family problems (84%). Other issues, such as addiction, grief, and guilt, were lower on the list. Ministers regularly encounter parishioners overcome by depression; it cannot be avoided.

Depression and Hope concerns what psychiatry refers to as *major depression.* Major depression, or melancholy or melancholia (all three terms are used interchangeably in this book), is not a passing feeling of sadness or malaise. Take Corrina, for example. She strides into the break room, pours a cup of high-test coffee, and exclaims to her coworkers: "This day is already a disaster. I got a ticket on the way to work—my husband will be furious, it's my third one this year—then I find out my secretary's out sick, the window in my office is leaking, I feel lousy. AND, today's the day Mr. Sotello is doing my performance review! I'm so depressed, I think I'll just shoot myself."

Is Corrina depressed? It seems unlikely. She has energy and a sharp wit. True, she is overstressed, and most of us would feel low, angry, or unwell in her situation. She says that she is depressed but adds a facetious tag line. It will pass.

The common symptoms or characteristics of major depression fall into four categories: interpersonal, physiological, cognitive, and behavioral. This book will describe these four groups of symptoms and suggest specific pastoral counseling interventions that address them effectively. *Accidie,* the dark night of the soul, spiritual desolation, *Anfechtungen,* or other spiritual struggles, this book claims, are not in a fifth category. Spiritual struggles are the whole of which the other four are components (chapter 2).

Depression and Hope is divided into two parts. Part One, "Assessment," presents an understanding of what depression is and, more specifically, what I mean by depression in this book, while comparing it to various spiritual struggles that resemble depression. Chapter 1, "Characteristics of Depression," describes the four categories of depressive symptoms: interpersonal, physiological, cognitive, and behavioral.

Chapter 2 looks at the close similarity between depression and spiritual desolation. It recognizes, in spite of our need to limit a definition of depression in order to talk about it, that in the Christian tradition there is a still-richer understanding of melancholia and a bright succession of spiritual directors within which the minister stands when counseling the melancholic.

The third chapter discusses one of melancholia's most tragic consequences, suicide. Assessment of suicide risk is so critical in counseling the melancholic that this chapter precedes any discussion of typical counseling approaches to depression. It describes ways to assess whether the depressed might take their own life and offers practical direction for dealing with the risk without delay.

Since it is a given that people who are depressed experience considerable suffering, chapter 4 considers the impact of depression on long-term intimate relationships, marriage, and family life; clearly, the depressed individual is not the only one who suffers.

How do we help people move from absorption with the past to a new view of the future where hope can be found? This is the focus of chapter 5, "Reframing Hope." It describes depression as a negative frame of experience, then offers a way for pastors and counselees to assess the negative frame and to reframe the experience more hopefully.

The chapters in Part Two, "Action," describe in detail how pastors can respond to depressed individuals. Chapters 6 through 10 present an approach to care and counseling for the depressed. Each chapter details counseling interventions that address the four characteristics of depression. Chapter 6 describes a pastoral caregiving process that is brief, as befits the actual time available to ministers in their counseling. Chapter 7 addresses interpersonal interventions; chapter 8, physiological; chapter 9, cognitive; and chapter 10, behavioral interventions.

For most depressed individuals in the church, parish pastors are fully capable of offering quality care in concert with the family physician. Situations arise, however, when referral for outside counseling is appropriate. The epilogue suggests positive ways for ministers to care for those melancholics to whom, for a variety of reasons, they cannot offer counseling.

Depression and Hope primarily covers care for those who will be described as mildly or moderately depressed individuals. The book focuses primarily on adults, although it would largely apply to adolescents and even some children.

Many people generously gave their time to read the manuscript and offer careful and thoughtful criticism. My sincere gratitude goes to Duane Bidwell, Mary Lynn Dell, Christina Hildebrand, Andy Lester, Rebekah Miles, and Susan White for their invaluable contributions to the manuscript as you see it. I also want to thank students in my classes at Brite Divinity School, who allowed me to test out many of the ideas presented in this book. Finally I want to express my deep gratitude to Karen Stone, who gave many hours of her time to reviewing the text and making it more readable.

For the past five years my research on depression has been assisted by a grant from Brite Divinity School, Texas Christian University. For that help, I am grateful.

Many of the ideas presented in this book are drawn from my day-to-day practice of pastoral care and counseling. Consequently the book contains elements of actual case histories. Since confidentiality is essential to pastoral practice, all case descriptions have been altered with respect to names and other identifiers in order to preserve anonymity while not distorting the central reality of the experience described.

A View of Depression

I am lost in an immense underground cavern with tangled, unending passage-ways. What distant light I could once see soon shrank to a glimmer and now is gone. Earlier I tried mightily to get out, to find the light of day again, but it is no longer possible and I no longer care. I'm very, very tired.

I don't have energy to turn back, to find my way out. It would be futile any-way. I have no real hope for the direction I am going. There is no real reason to continue but I am afraid to stop; I might never move again.

I am very cold. My hands are numbed by the cold, scarred, and caked with blood from my falls on the dark uneven floor.

People (those who wish me well and those who don't) are irritants. They want something from me, or they want to do something for me (which I do not want). I shudder at a knock on the door, the sound of the telephone. I wish all of them would be gone. There is nothing I want to do. Nothing excites me.

God is absent. Perhaps God has more important things to do elsewhere. . . .

Sharp words are now dull aches. The thoughtlessness of others is hardly dis-cernible. I stumble on. Cracking my head against an unseen rock brings fresh blood mingling with my tears. I hardly feel the pain. What was once acute now is only a dim, pervasive ache. Nothing matters.

Why should I go on? I see no light, no end, no way out. No one beckons me. All that exist are cold, damp walls closing in on me. Ahead is a useless journey, exhausted step followed by exhausted step, leading deeper into the unknown. Why not throw myself on the ground and let numbed sleep peacefully overcome? I blunder on.

These are my own words, penned in the middle of the night over twenty-five years ago. While I sat in bed beside my sleeping wife, my hand moved almost automatically. Thoughts became movement in my fin-gers, and I was merely an observer. The "cavern" was vivid; the bedroom was a shadow.

I was depressed. I had been so for several months and had several more to look forward to. My melancholy never reached the point of incapacita-tion; I functioned in my job, gave service to the community, visited friends, stayed married. But there was little joy. The images and the despair of that cavern dominated my inner world for a long time. I was one of more than 8 million people in the United States who, at any given time, are depressed.

Depression on the Rise

Eight million is a great many people; but even as you read this book the numbers (in proportion to population) continue to grow steadily. During any given year, according to a recent study, almost 10% of the adult population in the United States have significant depressive disturbances (Regier, Narrow, & Rae 1993). In another one-year survey, depression accounted for 565,000 hospital admissions, 13 million visits to medical doctors, and 7.4 million hospital days per year (U.S. Dept. of Health, vol. 1 1993, 9). Even twenty-five years ago, 75% of all those hospitalized in a psychiatric hospital reported depression as part of the cause of their treatment (Beck 1979). A Rand study of medical outcomes (Fawcett 1993) pointed out that only symptomatic angina caused greater physical impairment than depression, but depression came out highest of all disorders in terms of days in hospital beds. Suicide, a common result of depression, leads to at least 1% of the deaths annually in the United States—possibly more, since many suicides are not reported.

Depression is on the increase. The growth is global—a study of inhabitants in Western Europe, North America, the Middle East, and Asia recorded striking increases (Dayringer 1995, xvi). Depression's rise in the United States is happening so fast that the change is hard to interpret.

Are more people really becoming depressed? Or are they simply more educated about mental health issues, less reticent to admit to their depressive symptoms, more willing to seek treatment? At first I was suspicious about accounts of the rising incidence of depression, assuming that it was primarily a case of increased reporting. Now, however, there is ample data (including the cross-cultural studies mentioned above) to demonstrate that a fast-growing percentage of people are becoming depressed. Various studies report the incidence of depression has increased three to ten times since the end of World War II.

The research statistics derive not only from numbers of people in therapy or taking antidepressant medications but also from community studies in which researchers conduct door-to-door surveys. (Such surveys typically refrain from naming diagnostic categories but instead question subjects about specific feelings and behaviors.) The goal is to determine how many people have experienced depression at some point in their lifetimes. From such studies it seems evident that depression's rise is not only a consequence of increased detection or the greater willingness of people to undergo therapy (Yapko 1996), but an actual phenomenon.

Although the incidence of depression has been increasing steadily in all age groups, there is a noticeable shift toward younger individuals. Depression's onset can occur at any age but most commonly begins in the twenties or thirties. Over half of those who experience one bout of depression will undergo another; more than 70% of individuals who have suffered two melancholic episodes will have a third; and almost 90% of all who have had three episodes of depression will have another one or more (U.S. Dept. of Health, vol.1 1993, 73). For some people "the episodes are separated by many symptom-free years of normal functioning. For others, episodes become increasingly frequent with greater age" (ibid., 21). The majority of people who are depressed do not seek treatment. Those who do not get some form of help can expect their depression to last somewhere between 6 and 24 months.

Since it strikes especially during the adult, career-building, child-rearing years, depression affects not only the individual but also the marriage, family, church, and community. It is the "common cold" of mental and emotional disorders.

The Depressed as Church Members

What about melancholia in the church? Do clergy in their pastoral counseling encounter the same problems that mental health professionals address? Is depression the common cold of emotional distress in congregations as well?

A. E. Benner (1992) examined this issue. He asked parish pastors to name the five concerns most frequently brought to them by parishioners. Depression (reported by 64% of ministers) was second only to marriage, family, and divorce difficulties (84%). Also listed were addiction (44%), grief (38%), and guilt (37%). Ministers regularly respond to parishioners overwhelmed by melancholy. Like their secular colleagues, clergy must deal with serious mental health issues (Larson, et al. 1988; Hohmann and Larson 1993), and depression will inevitably occupy much of their counseling time and energy.

We have seen that depression is on the increase. If it were viewed as a physical disease, it would be called an epidemic. Is it possible that our culture is depressogenic—that it unwittingly fosters depression? The hour or two each week that individuals spend in church or in counseling is meager compared to the remaining 117 waking hours in which our culture exerts its influences. It may even be that many therapists, by their emphasis on self and feelings, by examining the past and dwelling on the problems of the present, actually *nurture* depression rather than strengthen individuals to combat it (Seligman 1990a).

If on average this melancholy, this inner barrenness, this dryness of spirit will be felt yearly by about one of every ten adults in the churches we serve, how will this affect their involvement in the traditional structures of church life? Will they even be in church? Is a depressed church member able to experience any hope, or only despair? Is depression tantamount to lack of faith and therefore sin? If the sermon speaks of faith, hope, and love, how can the melancholic—who has little faith in God or anyone else, lacks hope for a positive future, retreats from people, and feels that no one cares—extract any meaning from the trinity of virtues? Even more, what do these words mean when the very person speaking them is in the depths of melancholia? How can a depressed minister speak convincingly of faith, of the love of God and neighbor, and of the hope that we share?

These are serious questions. Some of them appear to be conundrums because all of the obvious solutions are blocked by the nature of the problems. But, in fact, answers exist to these and many more questions, along with whole or partial remedies to the countless problems of depression.

It is to these answers, and the hope they engender, that this book is devoted.

PART ONE | **Assessment**

ONE | **Characteristics of Depression**

Melancholia did not suddenly appear on the scene in modern times. Throughout recorded history one can find descriptions of depression and explanations for its cause.

The Book of Job tells the story of a heavy grief, an immense melancholy, a leviathan of despair. Job, the good man tested with more tragedies and misfortunes than seems possible in one human life, was at his lowest. In the depths of his anguish, Job could not imagine his life improving. He turned his anger from his parents to God: "God's onslaughts wear me away" (Job 6:4). He described his agony: "My eyes are dim with grief, my limbs wasted to a shadow. . . . My days die away like an echo; my heart strings are snapped" (Job 17:7-11).

What exactly is depression? How does it develop? From the earliest written descriptions of depression to the present, helpers and theorists have disagreed about the answers to these questions. Under some circumstances, such as bereavement, depression is a normal and natural response. Just as there is normal and pathological grief, so there is ordinary and morbid depression. There always have been melancholic artists and poets. In seventeenth-, eighteenth-, and early nineteenth-century England it was rather fashionable to be overcome with melancholia. In fact, low periods may be beneficial for those who are unhappy with the way they are living their lives; depression can serve as a signal that something is wrong and provide an impetus for positive change. For those who are grieving, it is a necessary part of the healing process.

Melancholia, the historical word for depression (used as its synonym in this book), literally means "black bile," one of the chief humors, or body fluids, which in ancient Greece was believed to come from the kidneys or spleen and produce depression, irritability, or gloominess. Even today we speak of "venting one's spleen" to mean unloading a verbal barrage of negative feelings. Hippocrates observed depression some 2500 years ago and opined that it arises from particular dyscrasias of blood and humors: "Melancholics develop their illness when the blood is contaminated with gall and mucous; their mental state is disturbed, many even become mad." In his discussion of one patient, Hippocrates wrote, "Stupor accompanies her continuously; loss of appetite, sleeplessness, loss of initiative, attacks of rage, discontent, expressions of melancholy affect." He did not equate momentary bouts of loneliness or feeling blue with melancholia but suggested only that "if feeling of fear or sadness continues for a long time, the suffering is melancholic" (Tellenbach 1980, 5).

Causes of Depression

Debate over the causes of depression has simmered for a long time. Is depression based on environment (psychosocial factors) or physiology (genetic, biochemical, and neurological predispositions)? Good rationales can be found for both perspectives. But it would be difficult to argue successfully that either environment alone or physiology alone generates depression, because the causes of depression are multiple. They vary from person to person and situation to situation. Some people may require few (if any) environmental precipitators to bring on a depressive episode; it seems to come out of the blue. Others may endure a series of troubles over a long period of time before succumbing to melancholy. Still others never experience it, no matter how difficult their lives may be.

Some counselees cannot identify what has triggered their depression. They may even report physical symptoms such as sleep disturbance and fatigue without being aware that they are depressed, even without feeling remarkably sad or down. In other cases, a seemingly minor environmental event will set off deep feelings of sadness and hopelessness.

A physiological component does contribute to depression, and it seems clear that certain endocrine and neurotransmitter disturbances affect mood. Recent research by Drevets and associates has noted that dysfunction in certain areas of the brain such as the prefrontal cortex is also related to depression (Damasio 1997). In depressed individuals the left side of the prefrontal cortex was smaller than those in a control group. What is the implication of this reduced size of an area of the brain that seems to affect the emotions? Antonio Damasio (1997, 770) writes that "the overall region identified in their study has been implicated in the modulation of neurotransmitters such as serotonin, noradrenaline and dopamine, whose levels are manipulated by antidepressant drugs. . . . These findings indicate that the human ventromedial prefrontal cortex is critical for the processing of emotions." From these and other studies, it seems evident that depression is the most physiologically based of emotional afflictions. Indeed some individuals, no matter how well they care for themselves spiritually, emotionally, or physically, experience depression because of their physiological vulnerability to it.

Indeed, this physiological vulnerability to depression affects some people more than others. You or I may respond to a scowl or angry words from a colleague with the thought "she's just out of sorts today." But for susceptible people even such a minor event can activate a downward spiral of self-recrimination, self-doubt, social isolation, and pervasive despair. The difference is not necessarily one of relative mental or spiritual well-being; it is in the person's physiology. It appears that in some cases depression is completely precipitated physiologically, in other cases it is caused only psychologically, and in *most* cases there is a mixture of causes.

If depression is at least somewhat physiologically based, should not the sufferer be given antidepressants rather than counseling? The answer is an equivocal yes and no. Research suggests that various forms of antidepressants are at least somewhat helpful for 65% of melancholics, but that leaves 35% who cannot be helped by drugs and others who are unwilling to take medication or who suffer from side effects that preclude their use.

Even if a person's depression has a physiological cause, it does *not* have to be treated by physiological measures alone. Pastoral counseling can be of benefit to most individuals regardless of whether one's depression is due to environmental factors or to a physiological predisposition.

Major Depression

The focus of this book is on what psychiatrists call *major depression*. Major depression does not mean feeling blue for a few days. It is not grieving a spouse's death. It is not the same as psychosis—the severe mental disorder in which individuals lose contact with reality—though the two disorders may exist simultaneously in one person.

Nor is our topic *bipolar disorder* (sometimes called *manic-depressive disorder*), but I will describe it briefly here. Individuals with bipolar disorder typically experience periods of major depression interspersed with spells of mania or frenetic activity. They may feel better and think they are back to normal when in reality they are in the manic phase of the bipolar disorder. During the manic phase, bipolar persons exhibit expansive moods, grandiosity, hyper-talkativeness, racing thoughts, and distractibility. They may be very impulsive and agitated (U.S. Dept. of Health, vol. 1 1993, 35). Typically this manic episode is followed by a return to depression. Ninety-five percent of individuals with a diagnosed bipolar disorder will have episodes of depression (ibid., 19), but because of swings from one extreme to another, their treatment is unique and outside of the scope of this book.

The depressive experience is complex, and there are many ways to view it. Mary Louise Bringle (1996, 331) cautions against oversimplification:

> The biological reductionist says, "Can't you just give me a pill and make me well?" The spiritual reductionist says, "It must be God's will that I'm suffering, so I've got to figure out why I'm being punished." The sociopolitical reductionist concludes, "If only I weren't living in this oppressive society I wouldn't have so much to be depressed about," and the sociopsychological reductionist laments, "If only I weren't in this bad relationship playing out all the destructive scripts from bad relationships in my past, I wouldn't be so unhappy."

All of these responses have the ring of truth, but none captures enough of it; they do not sufficiently explain the melancholic experience. They are "too unidimensional to account for the full complexity of our experience, but single strands are simpler to unravel than whole tapestries and tangles. In our weak moments, simplicity is seductively appealing" (ibid.).

That is one reason that (no matter how real the oppression of sexism, racism, ageism, and other forms of social injustice), in treating depression the focus is on taking responsibility—to the finite extent that it is possible—for one's own well-being. When oppression puts people in situations in which they are especially vulnerable to depression, blaming something or someone else for one's melancholia is too easy, too one-dimensional, too conveniently grasped onto by those who already have a victim mentality. Where oppression exists and contributes to depression, sufferers need to become active in the fight against injustice and not allow it to unravel their own lives. Remember that injustice is not only found in giant institutions on a scale that might be daunting for depressives to address; it also occurs in the grocery store, next door, within the family, in the church.

And depressives *are* in church, in considerable numbers (see chapter 2). Even within the community of faith, much of their suffering goes unnoticed or at least uncared for. Ministers as well as concerned laypersons need a broad understanding of depression, one that ties together various perspectives and yet sharply distinguishes its key characteristics.

Characteristics of Depression

Depressives report a number of typical symptoms. It is highly unlikely that any one person would exhibit all of them. One may experience ongoing exhaustion and difficulty speaking with others yet have no sleep disturbance. Another may feel immense sadness, a loss of satisfaction in what previously had been desirable activity, and frequent bouts of crying—but few other signs of depression.

It is important to keep in mind that some of these symptoms are also characteristics of physical diseases. Several years ago I saw a man who described low mood, constant exhaustion, diminished appetite, weight loss, and ongoing marital strife. He had a history of depressive episodes, but the rapid weight loss and his general "out of sorts" feeling suggested to me that his problem might be something more than depression or problems in his marriage. I urged a physical examination, which revealed that he had cancer and needed immediate surgery. Pastors are in no position to diagnose physical illness; it is best also to refer anyone with symptoms of depression to a physician for a thorough medical examination.

The characteristics of depression fall into four categories: interpersonal, physiological, cognitive, and behavioral. *Spiritual struggles* such as *accidie,* spiritual desolation, the dark night of the soul, or *Anfechtungen* (see chapter 2) are not a fifth category of symptoms, though they share many of depression's characteristics. When assessing individuals with depressive symptoms, it is important to look in all four categories. A well-rounded approach to pastoral counseling of people who are depressed means appraising their functioning in these different areas. To focus on one obvious area and pass over the others might miss a vital key to managing the depression.

Interpersonal

Melancholics view themselves, the world, and the future negatively. That negative perspective extends to interpersonal relationships, where they see little chance for positive change in the future. They also have decreased psychic and physical energy and therefore have less to give in relationships. They perform fewer of the little nurturing acts that people offer one another—fewer smiles, phone calls, greetings, or thoughtful comments. They can become angry at those around them. Irritability, neglectfulness in relationships, negativity, and lack of a positive future make the depressed less than desirable companions.

Some melancholics become extremely dependent. Feeling helpless and hopeless, they are more likely to rely upon others for what they believe they are unable to provide themselves. Other melancholics undergo a loss of emotional attachments—both the desire to associate with others and, because they have withdrawn from people, the actual opportunity to be in relationship. Melancholics who do interact much with people tend to have interpersonal problems. They may have difficulty expressing their feelings to others in a responsible way. They may find it hard to assert themselves or, at the other extreme, may erupt easily in destructive rage.

Depression can have a substantial impact on couple and family relationships; between 40% and 50% of depressed people who are married have family problems as well (Jacobson et al. 1991; Roy 1987). Often it is hard to determine whether depression causes family difficulties or vice versa. Depressive episodes are more likely after significant marital conflict, and people are especially prone to depression following the end of an important relationship.

Several studies indicate that problems in marriage or family relationships precede periods of depression (Ilfeld 1977; Beach & Nelson 1990). More research will help to shed light on this chicken-egg question, for one thing is clear: individuals with marriage problems are more likely to experience depressive symptoms. If a woman sees her marriage as unsatisfactory, she has as much as a one-in-two chance of being depressed (Beach et al. 1985; Weissman 1985).

Depression in parents can have a serious effect on children, and many children who have problems in school or are brought for counseling are found to have a parent who is depressed. Several research studies that directly observed parent-child interactions suggest that depressed parents respond to their children in a dysfunctional way. They appear less responsive to their children and less able to resolve parent-child conflicts (Field et al. 1990; Gordon et al. 1989; Radke-Yarrow et al. 1993).

Physiological

Depression has not only physiological causes but also effects. Depression's effects include a general physiological slowdown, which often accompanies depression. For me, an early indication of the onset of depression was my racquetball game. I could not move my body around the court or hit the ball as fast as usual. Before depression reached the point of "down" feelings, my body showed its impact.

Retardation of speech patterns is another common sign. The depressed may speak more slowly and at a lower pitch, and the severely depressed may speak in a flat, lifeless monotone (if they speak at all). Sometimes their speech is unintelligible. They tend to be exhausted all the time, even after periods of rest, and lack energy to do what is necessary to combat their melancholia. Some people endure persistent illness without a known physical cause, or suffer headaches, constipation, or diarrhea.

Anxiety accompanies depression for some but certainly not all. The coexistence of depression and anxiety has led several theorists to consider the two as one phenomenon—a mood disorder—not two separate problems.

Loss of appetite may also attend depression; the sensual joy has gone out of eating and the food may seem bland. Other people may eat more when they are depressed, bingeing on large quantities in spite of losing the sensory pleasure—perhaps even the taste—of food. There also can be a diminished appetite for sex; the severely depressed often totally lose their sexual drive and experience sex as an intrusion into their private world.

Finally, sleep disturbances plague many melancholics. Insomnia is common, especially waking early in the morning and being unable to get back to sleep. A few depressives, like monks experiencing *accidie* (chapter 2), sleep more than usual—as much as 14 to 16 hours or more each day. I have counseled people who would fall asleep at one or two in the morning, wake up just long enough to get their children off to school, and then sleep again until moments before the children arrived home.

By far the preponderant sleep disturbance of depressives is early waking. It is so commonplace that every helper faced with a person exhibiting some symptoms of depression needs to ask, "Have your sleep patterns changed? Do you wake up early and have trouble getting back to sleep?"

Cognitive

Depression affects people's thinking; they tend to distort and misinterpret reality. Mary Louise Bringle posits depression as a broad term to express the mental, emotional, and physical changes that occur to melancholic individuals. Describing despair, she writes, "I mean the particularly cognitive component of this experience—the assumption of hopelessness which begins from an experience of pain in the present and sees no way out of it in the future. Despair consists of a shutdown of the imagination and a set of conclusions that there is nothing I or anyone else can do to make matters better, so there is no use even trying" (1996, 333).

Depressed individuals have negatively distorted perceptions of all that is around them. In this regard, Aaron Beck (1967, 255) speaks of "the primary triad," or the three major disturbed thought patterns of a depressed individual: viewing *events, self,* and the *future* in an idiosyncratic manner.

Events. The depressed perpetually interpret events negatively, conceiving their interactions with the world and with God as defeat, disparagement, abandonment, and deprivation. They see neutral or even positive transactions with other people as failures.

Self. Cognitively, the depressed evaluate their own selves as lower or of less value than when they are not depressed. They commonly indulge in self-blame and self-criticism, followed by feelings of guilt. When compared to others, they find themselves wanting. Instead of recognizing the specifics in a context, they think globally—which, when mixed with blaming and a negative distortion of reality, can cause them to spend many of their waking hours in rumination (see chapter 8).

Future. Melancholics often find it hard to concentrate. They may be indecisive, spending immense amounts of time trying to make a choice, looking for the perfect solution or the only right path. They focus primarily on the past; if they view the future at all, it is negatively. They suffer hopelessness, view a future of continued suffering and pain, feel trapped. To them, time most emphatically does not heal all wounds.

In my personal and clinical experience, depressives perceive God and faith in the same negative and hopeless manner. Although faith is not based on cognition alone, the depressed tend to be especially troubled by doubts or lose their faith in God entirely. They have trouble saying with the psalmist, "My hope is in the Lord." A steadfast faith that could not be pried loose by untold earlier adversities, even tragedies, can crumble under the weight of depression.

The depressive's view of the world can lead to thoughts of suicide. If life looks like one long stretch of unending and unabated suffering—suffering that is due to one's own defects—a person may view suicide as beneficial not only to self but also to friends and family.

Two additional topics related to the characteristics and etiology of depression bear discussion here: grief, because of its many similarities to depression; and alcohol, because it influences and may exacerbate depression's symptoms and growth.

Behavioral

Depressed individuals experience a generally lowered activity level. In other words, they do less. They engage in fewer spontaneous activities. They may spend more time sitting, staring into space, idly watching television, leafing through magazines, or napping. If they practice spiritual disciplines, they do so without vibrancy. More often they abandon spiritual activities altogether.

Associated with a lower level of activity is the tendency to avoid or escape from the usual pattern or routine of life. When I am depressed, all of my daily activities seem useless, boring, and devoid of meaning, and I have my "Volkswagen van" feelings. I want to throw a sleeping bag and fishing tackle into a van and take off for the lakes or the mountains. I do not want any constraints; I want to get up when I want, fish when I want, sleep when I want, and do whatever I feel like at the moment. "I want" becomes a motif.

In his novel *A Green Journey*, Jon Hassler (1985, 44–46) provides insight into this loss of meaning in everyday activities. Randy is a depressed young man, recently married, who has trouble holding down a job. His wife, Janet, successful in her new job as a school secretary, puzzles over Randy's depression:

> Now and then, alone in the principal's office with little to do, Janet would turn Randy over in her mind and try to pinpoint the cause of his depressions. Was she at fault? Were his parents? No, his gloomy periods seemed to come and go without any relation to events outside his head. . . . How unlucky, thought Janet, that an apprentice realtor should lose his belief in property.
>
> "Janet, what does it mean to own property? What does it really mean?" . . . Such talk amused Janet at first, but then it got tiresome, his finding absurdity in every commonplace thing. Nor was Janet the only one who was irked. At the office Randy gave his father fits by asking what difference taxes and interest rates made in the larger context of life. . . .
>
> Granted, this wasn't a good year to be selling houses (interest rates up, employment down), but Randy couldn't sell Grade A milk to a goddamn creamery in the best of times, as Randy's father explained to Randy's mother in December when he fired him and arranged for him to be night cook at the Burger Skillet out on Highway Four.
>
> In January, Randy lost the Burger Skillet job, not because he couldn't keep up with the slow night trade, but because he couldn't see what difference hamburgers made in the larger context of life.

The depressed not only lose interest in ordinary activities; their abilities to cope with practical everyday problems are impaired. People who normally could replace a washer in a faucet, find a lost mitten for a child, or deal with mixed up orders at a catalog store, now find such tasks insurmountable. They may cry for hours at a time. They may act like they are giving up. They may attempt suicide.

Although the most common behavioral response is activity retardation, it is good to remember that there are a few depressed individuals who, instead of doing less, exhibit hyperactivity in aggressive or compulsive acts.

Grief

All humans suffer losses—whether through divorce, a long-distance move, the empty nest, retirement, physical impairment after an accident, or, most of all, the death of someone close. With each loss there is the possibility of grief. With the death of a loved one, grief is virtually universal. With grief comes some of the symptoms of depression.

But grief and depression are not the same. Grief is a normal response to loss; it is not a mood disorder. Through my own counseling practice, and specifically from research I performed at the Los Angeles Suicide Prevention Center among widowed spouses, I have identified certain dynamics of grief, which manifest themselves in those who have suffered loss (Stone 1972).

The seven dynamics of grief are: shock; release of emotion; bouts of depression; guilt; preoccupation with the loss; anger; and adaptation to reality. They do not necessarily occur in a linear progression; thus, one who comes through the experience of catharsis does not automatically go next to depression. But these dynamics are to be regarded as seven *major elements* of the typical process of coping with a significant loss and are listed in the order in which they generally appear.

Shock

In the first few hours and occasionally for two weeks or so after the death, the bereaved experience periods of shock. Often the pain of separation is so intense that the mind is numbed until later, when the loss can be faced. Survivors may act as if nothing happened or behave in a wooden manner while planning the funeral. In a way, shock is the mind's natural anesthetic against the enormity and depth of pain caused by the loss.

Release of Emotion

The period of shock is usually short, though it may recur, and following it the release of emotion—or catharsis—begins. The immensity of the loss begins to grip the bereaved; as one emotion surfaces others follow in a flood. Some people become hysterical; others express emotions less openly but feel them just as deeply. Although crying is a common way of expressing grief, in our society it usually comes easier for women than for men, and the absence of open weeping does not automatically signify absence of catharsis. We need to let the bereaved feel free to express their emotions in their own ways. At the same time we ought not to be frightened when strong feelings come out; it is a normal, healthy part of grief.

Survivors often want considerable time alone during this period and may resent company that is forced upon them. One man explained, "They kept saying you have to have people with you. I said no. I've got to face these ghosts. I've got to live in this house. Let me work it out." In short, those who are mourning must have the opportunity to choose whether to talk with others.

Bouts of Depression

After the funeral is over and acquaintances have gone back to business as usual, the survivors face depression, despair, even thoughts of suicide. Periods of depression are especially prevalent during the first six months, then they seem to come and go with diminishing frequency and duration thereafter. Most say this melancholy comes in waves, can occur without warning, and seems almost to possess them for a time before passing. It is markedly different from the dulling, unrelenting melancholy that afflicts the severely depressed.

Psychosomatic changes may result from the emotional distress of grief, and dramatic physical disturbances sometimes appear. When depression is dominant, there appears to be even more physical distress, illness, "nervousness," and the like. The bereaved need reassurance that grief is an emotion and, like all emotions, it involves physical changes.

Guilt

Feeling guilty is inevitable after a loss by death. Questions such as "Could I have done more for Mom before she died?" regularly arise, and guilt over something said or done to the deceased is common. People often dwell on painful events or angry words, reliving scenes and wishing they had acted differently. But there also is the possibility that guilt—usually viewed as a negative emotion—can become positive, persuading people to be more thoughtful and tender in their treatment of others. Whether guilt is about real or imagined events, it is a consistent aspect of bereavement and requires sensitivity and understanding from the helper.

Preoccupation with the Loss

The survivors can become obsessed with thoughts about the deceased. Typically it is not a constant condition but ebbs and flows. The bereaved may function normally at some times but at others seem unable to concentrate on anything. By the time outsiders have stopped talking about the one who is gone, the preoccupation can manifest itself in guilt-laden ruminations, intense loneliness, sleeplessness, hallucinations about the loved one, or even taking on the behavior and mannerisms of the deceased. All are a normal part of grief; only when the preoccupation becomes an ongoing obsession do problems occur.

Anger

Those who are grieving may struggle with periods of anger or irritability. The manifestation of anger by the bereaved usually means that one is beginning to come out of the bouts of depression and preoccupation and is becoming openly expressive again. Grieving people focus their anger on various individuals and objects—such as doctors, the ambulance driver, the police, or friends and relatives. Their anger may even be leveled at ministers—which may be seen as veiled anger at God. Questions like "Why did God do this to me?" or "How could God let him die?" are often raised by those struggling with anger.

It should be noted that the bereaved's anger may also be focused on the deceased, who in effect has "abandoned" the survivor. Such anger is rarely verbalized because the person feels guilty about it and tries to deny such feelings.

Adapting to Reality

In this final dynamic of the grief process, the futility of withdrawal from reality increasingly dawns upon the survivors, who now (we hope) go on as stronger and emotionally and spiritually healthier persons, better able to help others who face the same ordeal. Reaching the seventh dynamic of grief does not mean the bereaved will no longer experience any of the previous dynamics—they may struggle with them intermittently for years—but they are open to new possibilities in the future.

Depression and Grief

Over time, grieving people, through the nurturing and care of friends, family, and church, adapt to the loss and recover without the need of a mental health professional. Those who already are depressed when they encounter grief, however, are in double trouble. Depression plus grief should alert ministers to the risk of major psychological and/or spiritual challenges. As Welton Gaddy has stated, "Depression tends to cause persons to turn their attention almost exclusively to themselves. Enter grief and a vicious cycle begins. Grief provokes self-pity, and self-pity deepens grief. 'Woe is me. All of importance is gone. No one else ever has known such loss.' Grief!" (1991, 87). Depression plus a normal grief reaction can lead to a stunted grief (Stone, 1972). The depression hinders a person's ability to respond to the care that is offered at times of grief and can blunt the ability to express pain, thus prolonging and intensifying the period of grief.

A grief reaction can resemble the sadness in depression, but grief stems from a specific loss such as the death of a loved one. Not so with depression. In grief the bereaved may hear the voice of the deceased, smell his tobacco smoke, dream about him. Not so for depression. The grieving sometimes experience troubled sleeping patterns, but not to the extent of the insomnia (especially early morning waking) that torments the depressed.

For the bereaved, periods of sadness intermix with their customary mood. They may feel blue, but that low mood passes and their typical frame of mind returns. Gradually their periods of sadness recede as they adapt more fully to the loss. Depression is more of an ongoing state, though even melancholics may feel better during certain times of the day.

Those who are grieving weep. Weeping is less common among the depressed, though it certainly does occur. The bereaved go through a period of preoccupation with the person who has gone out of their lives. The depressed more likely are preoccupied with themselves. In grief, people respond well to the nurturing and reassurance of others. The depressed regularly interpret the concern and helpfulness of others as interference. Finally, people feel empathy for the bereaved—visit them frequently, care for them, help them in many ways while they are grieving. Depression is not as socially acceptable as grief. The depressed can be downright annoying; friends do not bring them hot dishes and Jell-O salads. Melancholics are not good company (often they are not even very nice), and they are likely to push church members away from them instead of graciously accepting their care.

Alcohol and Depression

Not everyone who drinks is headed for depression, and not every depressive uses alcohol. The fact remains that *alcohol is a depressant,* and the melancholic who uses it is taking a life-threatening risk. Alcohol accelerates and exacerbates the downward spiral.

For illustration let us return to *A Green Journey,* as Hassler (1985, 103–4) portrays to a T the vortex of alcohol-enhanced depression. Randy moved on to a job selling water softeners and did alright until the sheer meaning-lessness of water softeners overtook him. Faced with dismissal by the end of the week, he had a stroke of luck and sold a deluxe model (bearing a commission of $140) to an attractive single woman who was new in town. His wife, Janet, being away in Ireland, he drove to a roadhouse called The Brass Fox to celebrate,

> where he sat at a wobbly little table and ordered a beer and a hamburger. The sale had excited him, and so had the buyer. He wondered why he hadn't stayed for dinner. Because he was married, that's why: one thing often led to another. But why (he asked himself halfway through his sec-ond beer), why, if he was all that firmly married, had his wife flown halfway around the world without him? . . . She truly needed to be away because Randy was such a glum husband. Yes, and he was worse than that—he was a heel. If he wasn't a heel he would have gone with her—she had begged him to go. Poor Janet. She deserved a better husband. He was moody and irritating and probably dull as dishwater. He drank his third beer and ordered a fourth.
>
> He'd *be* better, damn it, he'd change. . . . Randy ordered his fifth beer. He liked beer. Beer lowered his spirits. He had come dangerously close to being happy this evening. Selling a softener to the classy Ms. Ecklund in her clean little kitchen had elated him. Elation was not to be trusted. It never lasted. Happiness was risky. Beer was comfortably depressing. He turned his mind back over his unpaid bills and his wretched behavior as a husband.

And so it goes. People who are already struggling with depression often have learned not to trust happiness. Alcohol cooperates by bringing them low. It affects the central nervous system and seems to increase the likeli-hood of depression. In one study, alcoholics were allowed for a very short period of time to consume as much alcohol as they wanted. In the pretest, 12% of the participants were depressed. After the alcohol had been con-sumed, 41% of them were depressed. In the same study, after a period of abstinence the rate of depression decreased. One researcher commented on these findings: "Depression is but one of the psychiatric symptoms of drug use, over use, and abuse" (Gold 1986). Several studies of individuals who enter alcoholism treatment programs have pointed out that the majority of alcohol-abusing individuals who are depressed see their symptoms leave within a matter of weeks after they stop drinking (U.S. Dept. of Health, vol. 1 1993, 46).

Does excessive drinking cause depression, or does depression cause the misuse of alcohol? This is yet another chicken-egg question for which there is no clear answer. Certainly the two are associated. In an evaluation of twenty-four studies on alcoholism and depression, it was discovered that between 10% and 30% of alcoholics also experience depression at the time of evaluation (ibid., 45). Some depressed individuals seem to self-medicate with alcohol.

Whenever the pastor offers care to depressed individuals, the use or abuse of alcohol must be assessed. If depression is the presenting problem, it is important to investigate the individual's drinking patterns. The challenge in raising questions about alcohol use is that many problem drinkers will deny there is a problem, thus one of the first tasks of counseling is to slice through their denial and help them to face their difficulties openly. It is best for even light or occasional drinkers who are depressed to consider foregoing alcohol altogether until the depressive episode has passed. For the depressed who are abusing alcohol, abstinence is essential.

Not every depression, we have seen, is alike. Melancholia does not exhibit the same characteristics in every person. Some may experience early morning waking, lack of energy, and lowered mood; others may ruminate from morning to night about a failed relationship, pull away from everyone around, and threaten suicide. But the four categories of characteristics of depression—interpersonal, physiological, cognitive, and behavioral—need to be reviewed in each case. Pastoral caregivers not only should assess all four characteristics of depression, they should also choose counseling methods that address more than one of them. Chapters 7 through 10, which discuss pastoral counseling of depressed persons, will each focus on one of the four categories of characteristics of depression and suggest counseling methods that specifically address those symptoms. By attacking the depression from as many angles as possible, they can increase the likelihood of healing, restoration of faith, and hope for the future among those who despair.

TWO | **Melancholy and Spiritual Desolation**

Depression disturbs one's most important relationships; for melancholics this may mean family members or close friends. For the mystic or hermit monk, and indeed for all faithful Christians, that most important relationship is with God. When people feel the absence of God, when they doubt, when religious ritual and service lose meaning, their experiences are very similar to the symptoms of depression.

Pastoral caregivers listen in a certain way to the words of those who are disconsolate, a way that is distinct from other helping professionals. To clergy and other professionals in ministry, despair, suffering, struggle, and adversity are laden with spiritual import, because reflection on the experience of melancholy and spiritual desolation can bring depth and meaning to those who are trying to be faithful to the call of Christ (Stone 1996, 125–52). This chapter will discuss several experiences that compare strongly to depression: the dark night of the soul, *accidie,* desolations, and Martin Luther's understanding of *Anfechtungen.* Each is distinct, yet, in the realm of the spirit, all resemble what psychologists call *depression.*

Dark Night of the Soul

"God, you are my God, I am seeking You, my soul is thirsting for You, my flesh is longing for You, a land parched, weary and waterless" (Psalm 63:1, New Jerusalem Bible). As in this psalm, the literature on spirituality frequently makes reference to the "dark night of the soul." The phrase comes especially from sixteenth-century spirituality; John of the Cross spoke of it (Kavanaugh 1987). It is a "purgative stage in the contemplative journey during which worldly life loses all its attractiveness and even the life of prayer dries up so severely that the self feels utterly cut off from God" (Bringle 1996, 333). It is a time of yearning for connection with the Other but with little perceived response. It is a period of aridity, and it ordinarily includes some flatness or darkening of emotion. *Dark night of the soul* refers to the experience of being alone, of seeking closeness and a connection that is not there, of being vulnerable and recognizing one's own finitude.

But the dark night of the soul is part of the journey of faith. The image of a journey has served as metaphor and symbol for religious experience throughout history. Pilgrimages—to Jerusalem, Mecca, Rome, Canterbury, Lourdes—have been undertaken by religious people out of duty, devotion, or a desire for healing. Spiritual dryness that may seem like the end of faith is, in fact, a natural and perhaps inevitable stop on the journey. Ultimately it can be a source of hope and strength. In fact, to most mystics the dark night is necessary. It comes well into the journey; what might prove the undoing of a new believer seems almost a final tempering for the mature mystic in the movement toward unity with God.

In the dark night of the soul, the sufferer sees or feels little in which to find hope. Hope resides only in the unseen and unfelt. Perhaps this is what the apostle Paul was writing of in Romans: "We know that the whole creation has been groaning in labor pains until now; and not only the creation, but we ourselves, who have the first fruits of the Spirit, groan inwardly while we wait for adoption, the redemption of our bodies. For in hope we were saved. Now hope that is seen is not hope. For who hopes for what is seen? But if we hope for what we do not see, we wait for it with patience" (Rom. 8:22-25).

Reading the Christian mystics, I doubt whether their dark night of the soul is either uncommon or radically different from our own spiritual struggles. To what extent is their experience common to all, though enhanced or magnified by contact with God? Some authors (such as Evelyn Underhill in *Mysticism,* 1955) place mysticism in a pure and rarified state. Either you are John of the Cross or you are not a mystic; there are no imperfect or preliminary forms of "real" mysticism. It is as if mysticism had nothing to do with the ordinary makeup of human beings.

Surely it would be a mistake to blend mysticism with an immanent view of spiritual life wherein God is a bosom buddy; yet I find it congruent to view mystical experience as a heightening and integration of more ordinary human faculties rather than an imposition on them or a replacement of them. The dark night of the soul may well be a form of depression but with specialized characteristics arising from its association with the absolute. And, no matter what the user-friendly "Church of Have a Nice Day" would have us believe, the absolute is dangerous.

Accidie

The dark night of the soul is not the only plight to oppress the spirit. Early in the Christian church, the desert monks began writing of a condition they called *accidie,* one of the seven deadly sins. The term (also known as *acedia* or *akedia*) has gone through several transformations of meaning through the centuries. Evagrius of Pontus (fourth century C.E.) described *accidie* as a struggle with temptations, boredom, weariness, and difficulty maintaining attention or focus which lead to a physical and emotional exhaustion. At first *accidie* was used to describe a state that afflicted the hermit monks; later, its meaning expanded to apply to all Christians. In English-speaking countries *accidie* has been translated as "sloth," which misses the mark. Today its real meaning seems to be a lost concept.

Evagrius was also one of the first to formulate a list of cardinal or deadly sins (Bamberger 1970). Originally he listed not seven but eight "destructive passions"—avarice, sadness *(tristitia),* anger, *accidie,* vainglory, pride, gluttony, and impurity.

Evagrius belonged to a community of ascetic monks living in widely scattered individual huts on the Egyptian desert some fifty miles from Alexandria. Before he joined the colony of ascetics, he had been an educated, lifelong city dweller. The minimalist desert life must have been a stark contrast to the bustle and sensory stimulation of the city, and Evagrius saw monks who entered life in the desert fall victim to *accidie.* He described *accidie* as a spiritual temptation that plagued hermit monks referring to it as the "noonday demon," a reference to the psalmist's "destruction that wastes at noonday" (Ps. 91:6). First, Evagrius wrote, the noonday demon

> makes the sun appear sluggish and immobile, as if the day had fifty hours. Then he causes the monk continually to look at the windows and forces him to step out of his cell and to gaze at the sun to see how far it still is from the ninth hour, and to look around, here and there, whether any of his brethren is near. Moreover, the demon sends him hatred against the place, against life itself, and against the work of his hands, and makes him think he has lost the love among his brethren and that there is none to comfort him. If during those days anybody annoyed the monk, the demon would add this to increase the monk's hatred. He stirs the monk also to long for different places in which he can find easily what is necessary for his life and can carry on a much less toilsome and more expedient profession (Wenzel 1967, 5).

Evagrius examined *accidie* throughout his writings. He concluded that the monk eventually would experience "dejection, restlessness, hatred of the cell and the monk's brethren, desire to leave and seek salvation elsewhere. . . . In the end *accidie* causes the monk either to give in to physical sleep, which proves unrefreshing or actually dangerous because it opens the door to many other temptations, or to leave his cell and eventually the religious life altogether" (ibid.).

The temptation of *accidie,* according to Evagrius, especially befell new initiates to the ascetic life. Life in the desert could be bleak, repetitious, and without external attractions. The transition from response to external stimuli in one's environment, to detachment from them and attunement to the internal relationship with God, led to the battle with *accidie.* (In this respect *accidie* is different from the dark night of the soul, which tends to afflict those who have been in a close relationship with God for some time.)

Evagrius counseled those who were grappling with *accidie* to "keep careful watch" of how it affected them—to pay attention to their thoughts and feelings. The ultimate goal was to "name the demons" and to become familiar enough to recognize the movements of *accidie.*

Although it seems likely that Evagrius was not the first to catalog the cardinal sins, the influence of Evagrius's list spread beyond his region and his time. John Cassian, a fifth-century monk in Marseilles, extended and clarified Evagrius's writings, especially the eight cardinal sins, and made them useful to later centuries of Christianity. Cassian combined *accidie* and *tristitia* into a single deadly passion (trivialized as *sloth* in the English translation); ever since, the catalog has been known familiarly as the seven deadly sins (Luibheid 1985).

Cassian believed that *tristitia* (sadness), like *accidie,* could occur "as if spontaneously," "without reason," having no "understandable cause." In pointing this out, Cassian seems to have been "attuned to the kind of free-floating depression which a person sometimes feels without being able to specify why" (Bringle 1990, 57). Cassian himself wrote,

> We feel overwhelmed, crushed by dejection for which we can find no relief. . . . [Our] train of thought becomes lost, inconstant, and bewildered. . . . We complain, we try to remind our spirit of its original goals. But in vain. Sterility of the soul! And neither the longing for heaven nor the fear of hell [is] capable of shaking our lethargy (ibid.).

Elsewhere Cassian stated that *accidie* causes "such fatigue and such hunger that one feels tired as if one has traveled a long way or completed a very difficult job, or as if one were exhausted by a complete fast of two or three days!" (ibid., 57).

This certainly seems like a contemporary picture of depression. Cassian's descriptions, based upon the previous work of Evagrius, give a clearer sense of the meaning of *accidie* and its impact upon the desert monks as they tried to stay faithful to their monastic task and their relationship with God.

How does one respond to *accidie*? Evagrius counseled a life of contemplation. Cassian added manual labor, tenacity, and endurance. And Gregory the Great, largely responsible for making the seven deadly sins applicable for all Christians and not just for monks, urged "spiritual joy." Gregory is quoted as saying that people become "gay or sad, not owing to circumstances but to temperament" (Davis 1950, 96). He seemed to recognize that some people have a predisposition to this depression-like state. According to Gregory, "the best cure for despair is an awareness of the possibilities of grace, a cultivated confidence in God's benevolence and ultimate benediction" (Bringle 1990, 60).

The remarkable similarity between Evagrius's description of *accidie* and a contemporary understanding of depression cannot be missed. It was a form of melancholia that profoundly affected one's relationship to God.

Desolations

Ignatius of Loyola, the sixteenth-century founder of the Society of Jesus (the Jesuits), described yet another similar spiritual condition: desolations. In *Spiritual Exercises,* he explained his method of deepening one's relationship with God. The *Exercises* were written and revised over a long period of time; his ideas for them germinated during his reading while he was in Pamplona convalescing from a war wound.

The ideas presented in *Spiritual Exercises* reflected Ignatius's own life and were intended to edify seekers concerning their journey of faith. Central to the exercises is a form of spiritual retreat in which Ignatius guided Christians through four time periods ("weeks") of meditations. The first week brings seekers to greater self-knowledge, especially of their sin; the second week enhances the retreatants' inner awareness of Jesus' invitation to follow him; the third week focuses on the passion of our Lord, attaining greater love for Christ, and discipleship; and the fourth week emphasizes the risen Christ and helps those on retreat to express unselfish love toward others. Service to the reign of God is the final movement of the meditative life.

One of the topics addressed in the *Exercises* is "consolations and desolations." Although those who use the *Exercises* learn about themselves throughout the retreat, the first week focuses particularly on self-knowledge—especially knowledge of one's sin. Self-knowledge, according to Ignatius, is not only about what we know in our minds but also about what we know in our hearts. At this feeling level, *desolations* may emerge as retreatants face themselves more honestly. Ignatius described spiritual desolations as

> darkness of soul, turmoil within it, and impulsive motion toward low and earthly things, or disquiet from various agitations and temptations. These move one toward lack of faith and leave one without hope and without love. One is completely listless, tepid, and unhappy, and feels separated from our Creator and Lord (Ganss 1991, 202) .

In short, desolations are interior movements away from God. It is hard to read Ignatius's description of desolations without noting the similarities to depression. Over the years various authors have disagreed whether the two are the same. Most believe they are not identical, though the affective experience of spiritual desolations can be very *similar* to depression (Loftus 1983). According to Ignatius, the key theological distinction was that desolations signify a movement away from God. People can be depressed without experiencing religious desolations; they can experience religious desolations without depression; or they can experience both at the same time.

Desolations, for Ignatius, presupposed awareness of the presence of God in one's life—especially the awareness of one's own sin and alienation from God. As John Loftus (1983, 173) wrote:

> Spiritual desolation for Ignatius is born in faith, only recognized by faith, and ultimately endured for faith. . . . It is not always a "dark night" sent by God as a temptation or testing to one already along the higher paths of spiritual life. . . . Desolation actually reveals the "not-God," the movement toward evil and death and faithlessness in each retreatant.

This religious movement can be clothed in very human forms. Depression is one of those forms.

Ignatius himself experienced desolations; he appears to have suffered from depression as well—even to the point of contemplating suicide. Ignatius scholar Constance Padberg states, "From July to October [1522], in one of the little rooms in the Dominican House, he passed through a terrible depression. The *Spiritual Exercises* describe what this kind of depression was. 'Darkness of soul, turmoil of spirit, inclination to low and earthly restlessness'" (cited in Loftus 1983, 187). Padberg discerns both depression and spiritual desolation in Ignatius's life—frequently at the same time. It appears that Ignatius's spiritual desolations had many characteristics that we would today describe as depression.

Even so, many people who experience spiritual desolations do not have significant, long-term symptoms of major depression, and it would be wrong to reduce spiritual desolation to the clinical definition of major depression. Yet it is impossible to ignore the many similarities between the two. On several occasions Ignatius of Loyola apparently experienced both at the same time, as have many others.

Anfechtungen

After the Reformation, the impact of the listing of seven cardinal sins upon the Church diminished. The reformers' (and especially Luther's) theology emphasized the human condition of sinfulness, rather than particular sins. In Protestantism to this day the seven cardinal sins have little influence. For Martin Luther, however, an *accidie*-like despair (which he called *Anfechtungen*) became critical to his theology. Like *accidie, Anfechtungen* has no English equivalent. Literally it means "to be fought at." The term refers to the despair, doubt, perplexity, and aloneness that humans experience. *Anfechtungen* is the recognition that God's commands cannot be met. It includes trials and temptations that can lead to despair. For Luther, *Anfechtungen* was a part of his struggle over the righteousness of God and the sinfulness of humanity. Eric Gritsch suggests that Luther experienced periods of "anxiety ranging from simple doubts to deep depressions, which he labeled *Anfechtungen*" (1983, 11).

Luther contended with acute bouts of depression throughout his life. "I myself was offended more than once, and brought to the depth and abyss of despair, so that I wished that I had never been created a man" (quoted in Gritsch & Jenson 1976, 153). "One may extinguish the temptations of the flesh" Luther wrote elsewhere, "But oh! how difficult it is to struggle against the temptations of blasphemy and despair!" (quoted in Bringle, 67).

Luther counseled that we should not let despair take over and run our lives; we should fight against it. But fighting alone is not enough. He also believed that *Anfechtungen* causes us to recognize our need for the grace of God. The "abyss of despair" brings us to our knees; from the depths of depression we learn of our need of God. Luther's own bouts of what appears to be depression helped him recognize his estrangement from God and his need of God's grace. In such suffering, the soul "is stripped of its own garment, of its shoes, of all its possessions, and of all its imaginations and is taken away by the word . . . into the wilderness" (quoted in Rupp 1953, 229). Naked and cold, lost with no hope, we are forced to acknowledge our dependence on the Other.

What remedies do we have for *Anfechtungen*—the existential struggles with despair or depression? Luther suggested several. Depressed persons must not let despair or the devil overtake them but fight back. They must oppose depressing thoughts and impulses with all their being. Luther advised, "Grit your teeth in the face of your thoughts, and for God's sake be more obstinate, headstrong, and willful than the most stubborn peasant" (Tappert 1955, 90). Instead of letting depression rule we must stand up for ourselves, fight back, and actively wrestle with it.

Luther offers a second recommendation for the depressed: enjoy the fruits of God's creation. Be happy "both inwardly in Christ and outwardly in His gifts and the good things of life. . . . It is for this that He provides His gifts—that we may use them and be glad, and that we may praise, love, and thank God forever and ever" (ibid., 93). We go out with friends, enjoy life, stay active, savor the fruits of the creation. Laugh, tell stories, sing, play games, go to the theater, enjoy a good meal, turn up the stereo and dance. We are not to keep away from others or deprive ourselves of God's gifts. Luther learned this lesson himself. Concerning his depression, he wrote that he had passed "all my former life in melancholy and depression of spirit, [but] now accept joy and happiness whenever they present themselves—nay, go in search of them" (quoted in Bringle, 70–71). Again Luther emphasized the active response of the one overtaken by despair. Seek out joy and happiness; do not wait for it to happen. And when happiness occurs (ephemeral though it can be), relish it. Enjoy it to the fullest.

Luther counseled that Christians oppose the torments of despair and depression in every possible way. All *Anfechtungen* are onslaughts from the devil. He proposed that we laugh at the devil. We are not to take the devil's assaults, such as depression, so seriously that they dominate our lives. Instead we are to live with our depression, as best we can, without allowing it to rule us—to mock it, refuse to take it so seriously that it wears us down until we cannot act.

Finally, according to Luther, the most important response of the Christian who is struggling with *Anfechtungen* is one of *faith*. To be depressed is to recognize that things are not as they should be and the future will not be as we would want. Luther understood that the answer lies in the Christ who went before us, who also experienced despair and desolation on his journey to the cross. Luther's theology of the cross provides the basis for a response to despair. We recognize that we need faith. In the midst of seemingly interminable melancholy and loneliness, lacking hope or any sense of a positive future, we trust in the gracious God who promises to be with us. No matter what we feel, our task is to hold on to the source of our salvation. We are made right with God *sola gratia*, by grace alone.

The experience of *Anfechtungen* forces humans to recognize the need for the grace of God. To give in to depression, to allow the depression to rule rather than to fight it with all one's might, is to abandon faith in God's grace.

My Greek professor in college once told me that he had never in his life felt the grace of God. No ecstasy, no foretaste of glory, no inner peace nor even calm assurance that he could discern. In the absence of affective experience, he held on to grace as a *promise*. He kept faith in the God who made the promise, though he had no emotional or psychic sense of it.

Those who are depressed have a tendency to believe their inner feelings—what David Burns calls *emotional reasoning* (1980). But contrary to popular wisdom, emotions are highly unreliable. The depressed must not confuse feelings with belief; they need some of my professor's tenacious hope. They must hold on to the grace of God that is the foundation of our hope and of our lives as Christians, to believe it, and to act accordingly. The Christ on the cross hears our anguish and responds to our cry whether we sense it or not. We must cling tenaciously to the God who "bears our griefs and carries our sorrows" (Isaiah 53:4)—like my Greek professor, like Luther, and like Paul, who also had an affliction that he could not escape. He also held on to God's grace, and it gave him hope in the face of evidence to the contrary. "Wretched man that I am!" he wrote to the Christians in Rome, "Who will rescue me from this body of death? Thanks be to God through Jesus Christ our Lord!" (Rom. 7:24-25), and a few paragraphs later, "If we hope for what we do not see, we wait for it with patience" (Rom. 8:25).

Discernment

Centuries ago, without benefit of antidepressant drugs or modern psychotherapy, there were Christian leaders who not only coped with their despair but also cared for others. Evagrius, Cassian, and Gregory the Great urged us to stand resolute against *accidie,* to endure, to contemplate, and stay active. To that, Luther said yes and emphasized, even more than his predecessors, trusting in the grace of God (whether felt or not) for grace is God's response to the *Anfechtungen* of despair. In the midst of depression, hold on to the source of salvation, our ultimate victory over wretchedness and despair.

In that grace we find meaning, without which we cannot hope. Without hope we cannot act. An active faith is neither a cure for depression nor a guarantee against its return—but as a source of meaning it makes hope possible. With hope comes the possibility and the courage required for acting in love and justice for others. We are called to live a faithful Christian life regardless of our biochemical tides, life situations, and spiritual struggles. Doing so also makes it possible for us to take concrete steps toward positive change in our own lives.

The desert fathers urged us to learn about our despondency and to act, and indeed there are times when we can help ourselves and deal responsibly with our depression. Luther urged us also to trust; there are times when we feel powerless to help ourselves. Then we rest in God's grace, believing in what God has done for us through the cross. These various paths are appropriate for addressing the dark night of the soul, the demons of *accidie,* the desolations of the spiritual journey, the anguish of *Anfechtungen,* and the bitterness of depression.

Clinical depression and experiences of spiritual desolation need not be intrinsically connected, according to John Loftus (1983, 147); "either experience can be generated and proceed quite independent of the other." The religious person may be spiritually disconsolate without sinking into depression. Likewise one may have depression without spiritual despair. Sometimes both occur at once, each triggering and exacerbating the other.

One task of ministers, as they listen to depressed persons, is to discern what is what, and offer care accordingly. The pastoral caregiver must always listen carefully for the quiet murmurings of spirit within the words of those who are describing their depression. Is it a plainsong? Is it a fugue? Is it a discordant cacophony? Pastoral caregivers listen to the words of the spiritually disconsolate and depressed in order to perceive which music they are hearing. And when helping them to make the cognitive, behavioral, interpersonal, or physiological changes necessary to address the depression, it is important not to forget those murmurings of spirit, for they may indicate the sufferings of one on the path of faith. A sensitivity to those desolations, born of one's own life in the spirit will make the pastoral caregiver more sensitive to both movements.

The dark night of the soul, *accidie,* desolations, and *Anfechtungen,* are not conditions exclusive to another age or to mystics and members of religious orders. Spiritual suffering does appear to be a form of depression, but with unique characteristics and an intensity stemming from its relationship with Ultimate Reality. Ministers and pastoral counselors are uniquely equipped to offer assistance and hope not only to the clinically depressed but to those whose voyage of faith has led them to the dryness of the desert, to the torpor of the noonday demon, to darkness of spirit, to the abyss of despair. If depression is on the increase, at levels never before seen in this century, then the antidote for the heart that hungers to know God is a hope rooted in the abundant grace of God. In that suffering we can serve as instruments of God's grace and messengers of hope.

THREE | Suicide and Depression

Desolation, despair, and loss of hope can be fatal. *Every person who is depressed is at risk for suicide;* there are no exceptions.

Counseling the depressed is a serious business made more serious still by the ever-present possibility of suicide. Three-fourths of all melancholic individuals consider taking their own lives. The majority of people who kill themselves—more than 60%—suffer from depression (U.S. Dept. of Health, vol. 1 1993, 9). Close to 15% of those who require hospitalization for their depression ultimately commit suicide (ibid., 26). The peril is immense.

Once it has been determined that a counselee is depressed, the pastor's urgent task is to determine the suicide risk. If any signs are present, immediate and appropriate action must follow.

Never underestimate a depressed person's desire to escape the pain. The agony of severe melancholy is so strong that many sufferers consider suicide the only way to find relief.

Assessing Suicide Risk

Surely no situation is more alarming to a helper than encountering a person who is or may be suicidal. With so high a correlation between depression and suicide, *all* counseling with depressed individuals needs to incorporate assessment of suicide risk. The pastor must determine how likely it is that the depressed person will end his or her life—to listen for indicators of the seriousness of suicide risk and to make judgments about lethality.

The following factors help one to gauge the seriousness of suicide threats (Farberow, Heilig, & Litman 1968; Stone 1993). These nine basic criteria are not used as a routine checklist, but internalized—the answers can be obtained in conversation with the potentially suicidal person.

Suicide Plan

The most critical element in assessing suicide risk is determining whether suicide is an indefinite threat or a specific resolution accompanied by a plan for how to go about it. How *specific* is the plan? How *lethal* is the method, and how *ready* is the means for carrying it out?

Obviously more and less deadly methods for taking one's own life are available. A gun is more lethal than some pills. A full bottle of barbiturates is quicker and more certain than a handful of aspirin. And now depressed individuals who use the World Wide Web are able to obtain complete information on how to plan a suicide.

Immediate action is required on the part of the helper if a counselee has spent time thinking in detail about how to commit the act—has formulated a specific plan, chosen a lethal method, and has access to the means—the risk of suicide is very great indeed.

Age and Sex

Is the person threatening suicide a woman or a man? Old or young or middle-aged? More women *attempt* suicide, but over half (55%) of successful suicides are men. The threat becomes more serious with age, especially among men. A man in his late sixties is four or five times more likely to commit suicide than is a sixteen-year-old girl. *All* talk of suicide must be treated seriously, however; people are not statistics. In fact, the incidence of suicide among teenagers has risen in the last thirty years, although it still is statistically lower than for adults.

Crisis

Has the person recently experienced divorce, the death of a child or spouse, or perhaps a debilitating illness? Crises triggered by loss or impending loss often bring about serious threats of suicide. People in crisis may consider suicide as a way of coping. If their pain is extreme and they have a specific suicide plan, the pastoral caregiver should make an immediate active response.

Meaning and Religious Involvement

Strong religious beliefs and regular involvement with some church or religious group provide emotional support, but also serve as social constraint against suicide. People who are not connected to any religious group or belief system are less inhibited from committing suicide. Again, this is only a statistic; deeply religious people also take their own lives.

Symptoms

Some of the emotional conditions that may lead to suicide include depression, psychosis, and agitation. Agitated depression is dangerous in the extreme; in this state a person feels emotionally low but is nervous, active, and intense, thus possessing the energy and drive to finish the act. The helper needs to look for complicating factors such as recent death or divorce, alcoholism or substance abuse, sexual deviations, and a history of suicide in the family (parent, sibling, child, or spouse). All of these conditions significantly increase the risk of suicide.

Resources

People who are suicidal often feel bereft of resources. Even with family and friends around them, they generally feel that they are alone and nobody cares. The pastor must identify people who can help them through the crisis—relatives, friends, church members, social workers, coworkers— and encourage them to be frank with others about the seriousness of their difficulties. If someone appears suicidal and immobilized, it is good to inform one or two of those resource persons of the suicide potential so they can actively communicate their caring. When people who are contemplating suicide feel that they are without resources, the pastor must act as the representative presence of the church, broaden their network of resources, and provide support as they grapple with their predicament.

Lifestyle

A person's style of living is a factor in suicide risk. Those who are relatively stable—indicated by such things as consistent work history, long marriage and family relationships, and absence of past suicide activity—have some measure of protection against suicide. Such things as chronic addiction, job-hopping or multiple marital partners, character disorder or psychosis, and frequent unresolved crises are indicators of instability. Chronic suicide threats happen only among unstable personalities, but acute suicidal gestures may occur among the stable and unstable alike. Both chronic and acute threats are potentially lethal.

Communication

Has the person stopped communicating with others? This may be a sign of hopelessness and thus indicate a more serious threat of at least attempting suicide. Look for subtle, nonverbal signs that one is entertaining thoughts of suicide (for example, ceasing favorite activities, making a new will, giving away cherished possessions); these are just as important as direct verbal threats. Unfortunately, helping professionals seldom see such indirect communication. Family members and friends may not even notice the signs of distress, but if they do, they can provide the minister with valuable information regarding the likelihood that the threat will be acted upon. Pastors who maintain ongoing contact with key laypersons may hear of people whose behavior indicates they are at risk and can then seek them out before they act on their suicidal impulses.

Health Issues

Those who are dying or obviously ill may be attracted to suicide as a way of avoiding pain. The helper should determine if a suicidal individual is facing (or fears) a serious disease such as cancer, an impending or recent surgery, or chronic illness. Some individuals have taken their lives believing that they were dying of cancer when in fact they did not have the disease. Therefore, when listening to depressed individuals, be concerned not only about real medical diseases but also ones that a person suspects exist.

All of the above indicators need to be taken seriously, but—except for a detailed and lethal plan—none of them is necessarily dangerous by itself. It is important to gather as much information as possible and evaluate the whole picture to see if a lethal pattern is forming.

The Minister's Response to Suicide Risk

Assessing the risk of suicide is only part of the task. The minister must also act. The incidence of suicide among depressives is high and must never be treated lightly. When dealing with the depressed, always suspect that the person may be contemplating suicide. It is important to ask direct questions concerning thoughts about suicide. Do not wait for counselees to raise the issue. Ask.

Take All Ideas about Suicide Seriously

This is the basic rule when dealing with even the hint of suicidal thinking. When a depressed person says, "I'm tired of trying," "Life isn't worth living anymore," "There is no way out," or the like, the minister should speak directly: "Are you thinking about killing yourself?" It simply is not true that talking about suicide will encourage a person to do it; talking about it in frank and specific detail (so that assistance can be offered) is far better than ignoring it.

Talk of Suicide

When people are contemplating suicide, their family and friends often ignore or dismiss their suicide talk, perhaps because it is too painful to consider. But the depressed need someone to talk to about their suicidal thoughts. Therefore ministers should prepare to address suicide before crises occur. Those for whom suicide is part of their own family history need to ask themselves how well they can respond to talk of suicide. All pastoral caregivers must determine if they are comfortable with the idea of suicide and with talking about it, *before* they are faced with a suicide crisis in their ministry. If they are not, immediate referral is critical.

Many depressives talk of suicide. Their comments may be subtle and thus misunderstood by family members until it is too late. Help the family to listen for statements such as the examples given above, or "You and the kids would be better off if I were gone," or even "I've been thinking I should give you these phone numbers to call in case anything happens to me."

People who are contemplating suicide not only express it verbally; they also act it out by getting their affairs in order, talking obsessively about death, wondering out loud what it's like to die in different ways, making a will after they have procrastinated doing so for years, giving away their favorite things, purchasing a gun, or talking with the family about how to dispose of personal property. Any of these gestures must be taken seriously, especially if they are new behaviors. Sometimes it is worthwhile to educate family members about verbal and nonverbal signs of suicide so they can attend to them.

After a minister has assessed the situation and determined that there is risk of suicide, the family should do preventive work at home. They need to dispose of all weapons and dangerous drugs—preferably getting them out of the house. This includes sharp kitchen knives and razor blades.

One who is seriously suicidal should not be left alone—not even for a few minutes. A family member or friend needs to be with the person twenty-four hours a day during the acute suicide crisis, which usually lasts only a matter of hours or a few days. (Many prisons and jails follow this principle; guards are on duty inside special "suicide cells" at every moment of the day and night.) If it is impossible to be with a suicidal individual at all times, contact the police or a local hospital with psychiatric facilities to discuss the possibility of hospitalization.

Suicide Calls at Night

Depressed individuals can threaten suicide at any time, but the most difficult cases I have encountered are those who call in the middle of the night. People feel more desperate, fearful, and hopeless at night when the people they might talk with are asleep. Ministers need to have a plan for handling nighttime suicide calls.

Recent changes in telephone technology have streamlined the procedures for dealing with suicide at night. There were occasions in the past when my wife had to put on a robe and knock at a neighbor's door to make an emergency phone call for me while I kept a suicidal individual on the line. Call waiting, caller ID, cellular phones, and dual phone lines resolve such difficulties. The emergency 911 service now exists in most areas of the United States, so a person who is seriously suicidal or has already made an attempt, such as ingesting pills, can be handled by a 911 operator. The dispatcher generally will contact police, fire department, *and* an ambulance.

In many cases (most, from my experience), after a brief telephone conversation with the suicidal person the minister can make an appointment for the first thing the next morning and does not need to do any face-to-face counseling in the middle of the night. After talking for a while, if it appears that the individual is more relaxed, two steps are important. First, make certain that your counselee will wake up a neighbor, friend, or family member who will be there the rest of the night, and tell that person the whole story. Next, work out a suicide contract.

A suicide contract is an agreement by the suicidal individual to contact the pastor, an associate, or the local crisis hotline (provide the telephone number!) before making any suicide gesture. In face-to-face counseling, I write the contract down and we both sign it. Over the phone, I request a clear verbal statement of agreement to the suicide contract. I insist that the person repeat the telephone numbers to be called in an emergency and restate to me the time and place of the counseling session the following morning.

Serious Suicide Risk

If there appears to be a real chance that a depressed person will attempt suicide, and talking has not altered this fact, more active intervention is required. At this point the minister is obliged to contact the family (even if this means breaking confidentiality). Inform the family of the suicide risk and suggest options: contacting their psychiatrist or counselor if they have one, going to a walk-in psychiatric crisis center such as can be found in many larger hospitals, or calling the police. They should not be afraid or ashamed to bring in the police; sometimes it is the only way to ensure the safety of a person who has temporarily given up on life. If the person has already inflicted injury or ingested pills, call 911 immediately.

If no family members can be found, the minister may respond to the crisis situation in person—but never alone. It is good to have an arrangement with several members of the congregation, elders perhaps, who will be available to assist on nighttime emergencies. Take one of them along. If there is any possibility of physical violence, drug or alcohol use, or access to guns, the police ought to go to the home with the minister. It is not unusual for depressed individuals to refuse help from anyone—family, friends, or pastor—and the police or local emergency crisis team needs to take over. This is not a time for heroics on the part of the minister.

Otherwise the minister must do anything possible to restrain a depressed person from committing suicide. (Here I am talking of suicide in the case of the depressed and not in cases of people with fatal illnesses who choose physician-assisted suicide to end their life. That is a topic for another book.)

The acute suicide crisis usually is brief; people have died who most likely would have been all right and gone on with their lives if only they had been prevented from the act for a few hours or days. The depressed believe their feelings of hopelessness, and thus are convinced that the future holds nothing good, and other people will be better off without them. They have difficulty making rational decisions. Their vision is narrowed; they see suicide as the only way to get away from their pain. It is not the only option. The pastoral caregiver's task is to help them see other options. With careful help and intervention, their vistas may reopen and the true range of choices appear. Life may not be easy, but it can have meaning. Death is not the only way to end suffering. Even the deeply melancholic, balanced at the precipice of despair, can rediscover hope.

FOUR | **Family Life of the Depressed**

When one person is depressed, many suffer.

Often the depressed are emotionally distant and angry, uninterested in doing things with others. Their melancholia may have come on over a long period of time, so family members may fail to connect their behavior with depression. Instead, they take it personally. "He's irritable all the time. There must be some reason why he is dissatisfied with our relationship." "She's distant, pulls off into her own world. Maybe she doesn't love me any more."

A study of families with at least one depressed member revealed impairment in a number of interpersonal functions required for family living. The affected functions included such things as communication, problem solving, and the ability to emotionally relate to others (Keitner et al. 1986).

Impact of Depression on Interpersonal Relations

Melancholic individuals, as we have seen, view themselves, the world, the future, and their relationships negatively. To compound the problem, their psychic and physical energy is low, so they have less to give to others. They do not tend relationships well—they may return a cheery hello with a scowl, refuse invitations, close the office door, eat lunch alone, eschew giving helpful comments and compliments. Their irritability, neglectfulness, negativity, and lack of a positive future make the depressed less desirable as partners and more difficult to live with. Imagine coming home from a hard day at work, wanting to put your cares behind you for a little while. Whom might you enjoy spending the evening with: a lethargic, irritable, reclusive person, or someone who has energy and interest in things and is upbeat about your relationship? It is not a hard decision.

Family members living with a depressed person can easily become distressed. It is not difficult to understand why, considering the worldview of the depressed. Melancholia has been likened to "a magnifying glass, highlighting all the normal problems of families and family members, making these issues seem more serious, and adding stressful and worrisome troubles of its own" (Anderson, Dimidjian, & Miller 1995, 1). For some family members the problem is living with someone who is negative or irritable most the time; for others, lack of intimacy and emotional support is most troubling. Still others are worried about being sucked into depression themselves. The mood of many family members, if they are not careful, can be altered by the mood of one. Depression seems to breed depression.

Family members are not always aware that one of them has descended into depression. They may think the person is merely "not herself." One study put it this way: "The depressed person's relentless focus on the negative aspects of life is perceived not as a consequence of depression but as a reflection of how he or she actually feels about marital and family relationships. Family members tend to interpret symptoms of withdrawal, fatigue, diminished libido, and anhedonia as reflective of a lack of feeling and affection or commitment to the relationship" (ibid., 3). If family members do not recognize the depression, they may consider the depressed individual ungrateful or feel themselves inadequate as family members.

When people first slide into depression, family members usually rally around them. They are supportive. They offer help. Here is a common scenario: A father is depressed. The mother tries to serve as a buffer between the children and her husband. She protects him from the children's demands as well as the expectations of the outside world. She may try to counter her husband's negative view with comments such as, "It's not as bad as all that" or "I'm sure things will work out for the best." She may take on more of the family responsibilities to ease the burden on her mate.

Once this wife's initial attempts to help her husband fail, she faces a crisis. She is not getting many of her needs met in the relationship. Intimacy is absent. She has no one with whom to share her own burdens and joys, because the once-supportive ear is no longer listening. She is probably exhausted, especially if she has many responsibilities outside the home or small children to care for. After a period of time she naturally becomes less attentive or protective of her husband. She has less to give in the relationship. She is vulnerable to slipping into depression herself.

If the wife or other family members do not recognize the husband's depression for what it is, they may think he no longer cares for them. They will cease to accept his moodiness and begin to view him as an impediment to the well-being of the family. If the depression continues for a long period of time, the wife will come up with ways of living that are almost independent of the husband. She may have an affair. The relationship will become chronically conflicted and unsatisfying to both. Some women in her position simply leave.

Marriage and Depression

Some theorists have insinuated that marriage is good for men and bad for women (Bernard 1972). Research on depression presents a different picture. Rates of depression are highest among single people, whether unmarried, divorced, or widowed, and lowest among those who are married, *regardless of gender* (Gove, Hughes, & Style 1983). More women become depressed than do men, but married women have lower rates of depression than women who are single. Likewise, single men are more likely to be depressed than married men.

The reasons for marriage's protective function in inhibiting depression are unclear. Several who have studied the phenomenon suggest that an emotionally close, supportive, sharing relationship may be a key factor (Brown & Harris 1978; Roy 1978; Jackson 1992). Such relationships allow for sharing of concerns; provide emotional closeness, strength, and sustenance; and appear to provide protection against the situational stressors that can precipitate or exacerbate depression. One study found that many of the difficult events in life that can produce stress seem to have less impact on those who are married (Kessler & Essex 1982). Marriage somehow provides people with a way to deal with the day-to-day *sturm und drang* that beset most of us in modern urban society.

But it also seems to be the case that a lack of rapport makes life partners *more* vulnerable to depression. Spouses in troubled marriages are twenty-five times more likely to experience depression than those whose marriages are not distressed (Weissman 1987).

Does melancholia cause troubled marriages, or do troubled marriages cause people to be depressed? There is no clear answer. It appears that between 40% and 50% of depressed people are also experiencing family problems (Jacobson et al. 1991; Roy 1987). On one hand, some theorists believe that depression causes marital dysfunction. The evidence seems to indicate that brief, acute episodes of depression do not normally produce long-term difficulties in the marriage and family, but when one spouse is chronically depressed or has repeated episodes of depression, the marriage is at considerable risk. Pastors need to recognize the risk and initiate preventive measures out of concern for both spouses and their relationship.

On the other hand, people are prone to experience depression not only when an important relationship ends, but also when they encounter problems in a relationship (Bloom, Asher, & White 1978). After significant marital conflict, depressive episodes are more likely with both men and women. Several studies seem to suggest that problems in marriage or family relationships are likely to precede periods of depression (Ilfeld 1977; Beach & Nelson 1990).

This correlation is the reason it is important to stay alert to the fact that many people *suffer both depression and marriage discord at the same time.* When individuals speak to you of family problems, look for evidence of depression. When individuals describe depressive symptoms, carefully assess the status of their marriages.

Depression affects marriage not only while individuals are depressed but, it appears, in the aftermath of an episode as well. The family may not immediately return to effective functioning. Children or adolescents may act out; the marriage is at greater risk for separation or divorce. As Prince and Jacobsen state, "Some clinicians have suggested that the presence in parents of affective illness may be more detrimental to child development than are the schizophrenic disorders" (1995, 382–83).

To summarize: Married individuals experience less depression than those who are single. Married people who are able to be emotionally close, to support each other, and to communicate effectively, are protected to some degree against depression. On the other hand, marital difficulties increase the chances that a spouse will have depressive symptoms. Indeed, if a woman sees her marriage as unsatisfactory, the chances of her being depressed are as high as one in two (Beach, Sandeen, & O'Leary 1990; Weissman 1987; Weissman & Klerman 1985). Whenever a spouse experiences depression, the marriage is at greater risk for dysfunction.

Gender Differences

When it comes to depression, men are more likely to be in the role of supportive spouse; at any one time between 4.5% and 9.3% of women, and 2.3% to 3.2% of men, are depressed. (Earlier in this century women experienced three times more depression than men; increasing equality between men and women is beginning to include depression.) The gender difference occurs not only in the United States, but in a variety of other cultures throughout the world (with the exception of some developing countries like Zimbabwe, New Guinea, and Iraq). Depression is especially common for women in their thirties and forties.

Why are women depressed more than men? Again, there are no clear answers. One hypothesis is that the distinction is due to *biological/chemical/genetic* differences between men and women. Hormonal dissimilarity and changes in progesterone and estrogen have been the most common explanation among those who propose the biological/chemical/genetic theory. A relatively equal number of boys and girls who have not gone through puberty experience depressive disorder, but after puberty girls make up two-thirds to three-fourths of melancholic children (U.S. Dept. of Health, vol. 1 1993, 40). So far, studies of daily mood and the menstrual cycle have not shown a clear, significant connection between the two, although this explanation cannot be completely disregarded (Abplanap, Donnelly, & Rose 1979).

A second theory for higher rates of depression among women is *societal*. According to this view, women experience depression due to the power differential in sexist societies. Christie Neuger puts it this way: "Women and men live in a culture that is powerfully depressogenic for women" (1991, 150). According to some theorists, women's gender-role socialization causes them to devalue themselves, making them susceptible to depression (Chafetz 1979). Our society is patently sexist and oppressive of women. Research has yet to show that gender oppression leads to depression, however. It will be necessary to discover why other oppressed groups do not experience similarly elevated levels of depression. Research also will have to demonstrate why women in some developing countries, such as Zimbabwe and Iraq (which offer them even fewer personal rights), have a lower incidence of depression than do women in North America and western Europe.

Psychological rationales provide a third explanation for the phenomenon. Even though women handle stress differently than do men, studies of stressors have not sufficiently verified this possibility because women do not describe greater stress than men. Their perception of stressful life events is similar to that of men (Uhlenhuth et al. 1977). A more promising psychological answer has to do with coping style. Researchers have discovered that women react differently to their own feelings than do men. "Women tend to ruminate about the causes of their distressed mood, whereas men tend to engage in activities designed to distract themselves from their depressed mood" (Beach, Sandeen, & O'Leary 1990, 15). Women often brood over their difficulties and examine their feelings, while men are somewhat more likely to go outside and shoot baskets.

There is no decisive evidence that reveals why women experience depression more than men—only that they do. Ministers should be attentive to this difference in their pastoral caregiving for depressed individuals and families.

Children and Adolescents

It is not hard to imagine the impact on children of a depressed parent. Depressed parents respond to their children in a dysfunctional way; they are less responsive to them and less able to resolve parent-child conflicts (see chapter 1).

Many children who are brought for counseling or who experience problems in school have a parent who is depressed (Anderson, Dimidjian, & Miller 1995). Indeed, children of a depressed parent are more likely to develop depression themselves (Hammen et al. 1990). Conversely, treating a parent's depression helps resolve children's depression in many cases.

Several researchers estimate that upwards of 10% of children and adolescents have at least one depressive episode (Goldberg 1995; Kazdin 1989). It is difficult to pin down the incidence of depression among children and adolescents because they do not always exhibit the blue mood so common in adult depression and therefore do not report it to helpers. Parents, teachers, and even playmates are more likely to observe their subtler symptoms. Children and adolescents often display their depression by acting out. Some quietly withdraw from people and events. They become moody and irritable. Their grades may go down and they have difficulty generating energy for school or extracurricular activities. Children's depression also manifests itself in discipline problems at school, truancy, scrapes with the law, physical illness, and suicide attempts. Determining whether a child under age twelve is depressed or just painfully shy can be a daunting task, unless the child was formerly outgoing. In such cases consultation or referral to a therapist who specializes in family counseling or child psychology is needed.

Teenagers are more likely to express symptoms typical for adult melancholia such as sleep disturbance, eating disorders or lack of interest in eating, cognitive hopelessness, and lack of hope for the future. Even for those who are not depressed, adolescence is a moody time of life. One day the adolescent may be up and excited; the next day, down, grudging, and negative. The parents' job is to differentiate between the natural moodiness of adolescence and actual depression. The possibility of drug use can complicate it even more because some illicit drugs produce symptoms similar to depression. Unless the depression is severe, the distinction is difficult to make.

Adolescence is a time of breaking away from the family and gaining greater independence. When adolescents suffer depression, it is easy for parents to want to protect them as they would protect a sick child, yet adolescents need to break parental ties. Depressed adolescents need to express their freedom and individuality, and their parents need to allow them to do so. Frequently pastoral caregivers can help parents and adolescents negotiate realistic freedoms and boundaries. This is always done with the realities and the extent of the depression in mind. Parents must still be parents and take action (such as hospitalization or the prevention of suicide) if the depression becomes severe. In such cases, consultation with mental-health professionals or referral for treatment is usually essential.

Experience bears witness to the truth of this chapter's opening line: when one person is depressed, many suffer. Nowhere is this suffering more acute than in those closest to the depressed—spouses, parents, children. They share the same home, and they are held together by bonds of law, affection, and birth. They cannot escape the effects of melancholia, which spread like a slow-growing virus.

Marital discord is perhaps the most noticeable effect; in fact, about half of depressed people are in troubled marriages. The question of which comes first—depression or marital problems—has no clear answer unless it is "both." The depressed put an enormous strain on their spouses, who eventually may pull back from the relationship or succumb to depression themselves.

It is also evident that stable marriages act as a deterrent to depression. In fact, those in troubled relationships are twenty-five times more likely to experience depression than are those whose marriages are mutually supportive and caring. Pastoral carers need to assess each instance of marital discord or depression, since a great many people suffer from both at the same time.

Since women experience depression at a rate nearly two times greater than men, husbands more often are the caregivers. As we have seen, no one knows exactly why women experience more depression, though they do encounter biological stressors that do not affect men. Other theories include societal oppression and women's tendency to ruminate over their feelings.

Children suffer deep and sometimes permanent effects when a parent is depressed. It is difficult to diagnose depression in the very young, because they manifest melancholia somewhat differently than do adults. Adolescents are subject to normal mood swings and a need for independence that makes their depression hard to recognize and treat as well.

Clearly it is necessary to work within a family system when one member is depressed. All are affected and in need of care and direction. The minister who facilitates positive change in one part of the system is likely to witness improved interactions and renewed hope for the future of the individual, the marriage, and the entire family.

FIVE | **Framing Hope**

"**F**or in hope we were saved. . . . If we hope for what we do not see, we wait for it with patience." (Romans 8:23, 25) Hope is anticipation of the future, a sense that troubles can end or will at least become manageable, a recognition of possibilities that lie ahead, an investment in a future that holds promise.

In his book, *Hope in Pastoral Care and Counseling,* Andrew Lester writes of hope as the "trusting anticipation of the future based on an understanding of a God who is trustworthy and who calls us into an open-ended future" (1995, 62). Hopelessness is the perspective of most depressed individuals; those who feel hopeless have little sense of a worthwhile tomorrow—in Lester's words, a "positive future story."

Søren Kierkegaard's understanding of persons—for our purposes depressed persons—also helps us understand hope. In *The Sickness unto Death,* he describes persons as possessors of actuality, freedom, and possibility. All three are part of the authentic self, and a good relationship of all three is necessary for authentic existence. *Actuality* refers primarily to the past; it includes our context, our physiological predispositions, and choices we have previously made.

Freedom is what we have in the present. It is a finite freedom, exercised within the limits of our situation and abilities, our givens and past choices. Because of our actualities we cannot simply become whatever we want to be "if we try hard enough for it." We make choices, and act, from the range of options available to us.

Possibility addresses the future. It is what we can become as we use our freedom. In that respect our possibilities are not predetermined. We are not automatons. We can imagine, and within the givens of life we can become something new. Living as an authentic self, according to Kierkegaard, means looking beyond our immediate necessities or past liabilities. We anticipate the future with the awareness that we are free—however limited—to actualize whom we ought to become as faithful Christians and to take responsibility for shaping that future.

In short, faithful Christian living requires recognition of givens from the past and exercise of finite freedom in the present, so that positive future possibilities can be imagined and brought into existence. Those who are depressed, viewed from Kierkegaard's understanding of persons, allow their actuality (past) to limit and dominate their possibility (future) by not exercising their finite freedom in the present. So the anguish of depression comes not only from dwelling on a negative past but also from the loss of a positive future. Unfortunately, much counseling offered to the depressed focuses on actuality, on the past. It is a grave error. The purpose of the minister giving care to the depressed is to engender a hope that recognizes actuality but also steps directly into the future by exercising freedom in the present, by taking action.

The good news is that there are care and counseling methods that can engender future hope in melancholic individuals. Methods especially useful for enlivening hope include searching for exceptions, reframing, focusing on people's strengths, and creating future goals as a way to move away from preoccupation with the past.

Exceptions and Hope

Melancholics seeking counseling tend to think that their problems are endemic to their being. They do not notice when a problem is absent, or if they do they dismiss it as accidental. Steve de Shazer calls these absences *exceptions*—"whatever is happening when the complaint is not" (1988, 53). Two parents, for example, may claim that their son "beats up on his sisters all of the time." Though any violence should be taken seriously, the son is not literally being violent "all of the time." De Shazer (1991, 58) suggests that

> problems are seen to maintain themselves simply because they maintain themselves and because clients depict the problem as *always happening*. Therefore, times when the complaint is absent are dismissed as trivial by the client or even remain completely unseen, hidden from the client's view. . . . For the client, the problem is seen as primary (and the exceptions, if seen at all, are seen as secondary).

In pastoral counseling of depressed individuals, the *exceptions are of primary importance and can serve as the central focus of the counseling*. Here the pastor spotlights not the moments (hours, days, weeks, months) when the person is feeling depressed, but those times when the depression lessens or is absent, those instances of peace or quiet happiness or even joy.

The pastoral caregiver becomes a detective, digging out and pursuing exceptions by asking new kinds of questions (O'Hanlon and Weiner-Davis 1989), such as: "What is different about the periods when you are not depressed?" "How did you achieve that?" "What is it like?" "Did your spouse, family, or friends notice the difference?" "How could you tell that they noticed?" "How did you lessen the depression?"

Use compliments. For example, the pastoral caregiver might say to a depressed spouse: "I am impressed that you did not go into a funk last weekend when your husband came home late. How did you do it?" The minister calls attention to the one time when she did *not* go into a depressive spiral after her husband did not act as she wanted. She emphasizes a time of strength rather than her times of difficulty. Always phrase "I am impressed" statements in the present tense even if the incident occurred a long time ago.

Assign homework tasks. In the case of a couple that argues, the homework might be: "In the coming week, observe whatever happens between you and your spouse that you want to continue happening." When counselees discover exceptions to the problem, urge them to do more of whatever they did. These exceptions become homework tasks. The assignments do not propose new behavior to counselees, but urge them to do more of what they are already doing right. Focusing on exceptions generates hope.

Questions about relative influence help *externalize* the impact of depression. When conversing with counselees, ask "How has depression affected you?" or "What influence has depression had upon your life or the life of your family?" This method, developed by Michael White (1989, 8), encourages people to "map the influence of the problem in their lives and relationships" and to "map their own influence in the 'life of the problem.'"

Counselees who talk about the effect that depression has upon them and those around them open up new areas of their life for conversation, which at the same time opens up the possibility for exceptions to be discovered. Design questions to elicit memories of times when depression's impact on their lives was not so great, for example:

"Tell me about a time when your down feelings didn't rule your life so much. Give me another example."

"Many people have told me in counseling about times that they have been able to conquer their depressed feelings. Tell me about the last time you were able to keep them away, even if only for a few hours."

"You were able to stand up to your depressed feelings. Is this something that surprised you about yourself?"

"Tell me how this situation was different from times when depression was dominating your life more. What was the difference?"

Such questions distance depressed individuals from their melancholia and give them a chance to discover times when depression loosened its hold on their lives.

Framing Hope

By seeing the whole of one's life, the good times as well as the low times, a person can begin to recapture hope. Indeed, depression is very much like a projective psychological test. In the Thematic Apperception Test (TAT), for example, subjects look at a test picture and project onto it their own perceptions of what is happening. If the TAT picture shows a person standing and looking out a window, some viewers will say the person is looking out at a beautiful sunrise, peaceful and ready to meet the day. Others say the person is looking out into the dark, feeling lost and alone, feeling that no one cares.

Likewise people project their own frame of reference onto ambiguous situations. Life, of course, is an ambiguous situation from beginning to end. Some people project that life is good, while for others it is a pain to be endured "and then you die." The task in pastoral caregiving is to help individuals frame hope where they are now framing hopelessness. It is to help them bring their predepression faith back into their frame. When not depressed, many individuals speak of the comfort they get during hard times from knowing that God is with them in all they do. When depressed, people's awareness of God's being "with us" at all times slides from understanding. It slips away. The pastoral caregiver's task is to help counselees to reclaim a hope grounded in faith.

When we listen to people talk about their lives, we hear their projections. Depression is not the only way to interpret life's experiences (including its troubles). To illustrate: Bill, a counselee, stops by a friend's house and she is not there. He wonders why. In the ambiguity of the situation he can create many theories concerning why she is away.

Positive: *"She's out getting my birthday present."*
          "She is running and trying to stay in good shape."
Neutral: *"She's not home from work yet."*
          "Maybe her mother is ill again."

Negative: *"She is out with someone else instead of me."*
          "She doesn't really like me."
          "She never really cared for me."
          *"I'm a loser with women. I'll never have a meaningful
          relationship."*

Which of the above explanations is correct? We don't know. One of the tasks of counseling depressed individuals is to teach them to get accurate information rather than believing their projections. They have to learn to gather data and base their assumptions about experiences on that data. In a friendly way Bill can ask his friend where she was so he can know rather than project. He has to recognize his tendency to view events negatively and learn to suspend his interpretation of events until he has enough information to make reasoned interpretations. Indeed, he can learn to view ambiguous situations positively in order to counterbalance his negative slant (Seligman 1990).

Melancholic people need to develop tolerance for ambiguity. This is a formidable task since the inability to do so is a common feature of depression. Sometimes counselees learn to accept ambiguity by obtaining whatever information they can and then making decisions based upon whatever data exists. In other cases they learn, like Bill, to recognize that on many occasions there is not enough accurate data to make immediate interpretations. They need either to wait or to choose to view events optimistically— to become hope framers rather than depression framers.

To Comprehend Is to Form Meaning

It is virtually impossible for humans to perceive without interpreting. Most Westerners could not interpret a Burmese text, for instance, because its unfamiliar script offers not even the occasional cognate or proper noun to hint at its content. In this case the innate human impulse to interpret, and therefore participate in the meaning of everything we perceive, is frustrated. To *comprehend* at any level is to form meaning out of perception.

The depressed perform something akin to self-hypnosis when they form meaning out of perception: they continually tell themselves and others how depressed they feel and how badly their lives are going. Repeatedly they frame their perceptions in a negative way and form malignant meanings for most of the stimuli in their environment. John Walter and Jane Peller call these "symptomatic trances" which deepen with each retelling (Yapko 1989). Hurtful memories and real or imagined wrongs proliferate.

(Small wonder that psychotherapies which focus primarily on past events are not particularly successful in treating depression; the malignant trance is only deepened.) If this symptomatic trance is not addressed early in counseling, little change will ensue. Therefore one of the first tasks of counseling with the depressed is to reframe—to replace this negative induction with a more positive and hopeful perspective.

I offer an example from my own experience. Early in my career I was pressed into service as the director of a pastoral counseling center when the previous director resigned unexpectedly. The next month, when bills were due, I found the agency's finances in far worse shape than I had been told; in fact we had only enough money to pay half of the bills and salaries. (My own salary was often paid late in the year to follow.)

Initially, I viewed the situation through a negative frame. I was upset and discouraged at having to deal with the financial woes of the pastoral counseling center on top of learning to be an administrator and working full-time as a pastoral counselor, all for the first time.

A friend helped me reframe the situation. She observed that I could sit around and complain about it, or I could view it as an opportunity to learn new skills in management, finance, and fundraising. In a perfect world I might not choose to learn those skills, but they could be very useful to me in a number of ways. This new frame was not very exciting to me and I resisted it, but she reasoned that the more I learned about finance, the more it might help me with my personal economics, which she knew were also a little shaky at the time. I could not bring myself to embrace the agency's predicament as a "golden opportunity," though in retrospect I see it was; I only shifted my perspective enough to take on a difficult task with sufficient energy to help guide the agency back to financial health. I engendered hope by reframing the problem into an opportunity. In the bargain, I was able to put my personal finances in order and begin financial planning for retirement.

Every person of faith has a worldview. Key to that view is one's image of God. Melancholics generally have negative images of God as angry, distant, uninterested, incapable of helping, concerned about other things, weak, mean-spirited, not listening, chastising, and so forth. They interpret that whatever happens to them occurs because of this negative God. The pastor needs to help counselees claim more positive images of God, to reinterpret the events of their lives from the perspective of a positive God image. Depressed individuals need to apprehend a loving God who is actively involved in the world and in their lives.

To comprehend, again, is to form meaning out of every outside stimulus—to interpret neutrally, for good, or for ill. Even serious problems can be an opportunity for growth and greater strength.

Reframing Hope

Reframing turns liabilities into strengths. It constructs for people a new way to organize and view their experiences—not through rose-colored lenses, but through the clear glass of reality. Frames are the ways we perceive events or circumstances, and they shape our reality. They may be compared to patterns or templates by which we put together and interpret information and occurrences. The meaning of an event depends upon the frame of the person experiencing it. As meanings change, individuals can react to similar situations with very different feelings, thoughts, behaviors, and attitudes in response to the same or similar situations.

Reframing is a counseling method developed somewhat independently by several clinicians, most of whom were doing family therapy in the 1970s and 1980s (Bandler & Grinder, 1979; Watzlawick, Weakland, & Fisch 1974). It involves the initial acceptance of clients' problems (and their beliefs about them) at face value. To reframe, explain Watzlawick and associates, is to reinterpret an experience cognitively or emotionally in a way that fits the facts of the situation as well or even better, thereby changing its entire meaning (1974, 95). By offering a different, more positive interpretation of experience, the helper suggests another way of perceiving it.

Reframing helps depressed people look for exceptions to the premises underpinning their negative point of view. Once they entertain even the slightest doubt about any portion of their frame—once they consider that there may be another way of looking at the event—they find it hard to return to their previous point of view. They begin to visualize a future without the problem.

In an interview for *The Christian Century*, Parker Palmer (1995, 327) offered an example of reframing when he described his own battle with depression as a school of the spirit. His spiritual director suggested, "You can keep imaging depression as the hand of an enemy trying to crush you. But what about thinking of it instead as the hand of a friend trying to press you down to firm ground on which it's safe to stand?" Palmer described how that new frame helped him to see his melancholy and his relationship with God differently. "God as ground has become a very powerful image for me. God is that which will not let you down. If you feel yourself falling, it's probably because you started someplace other than God—someplace off the ground."

Describing depression not as an enemy but as a friend trying to press you down to firm ground is a good example of reframing depression.

Pastoral caregivers certainly do not want to leave depressed counselees with the impression that an angry God is bringing upon them the blight of depression because of their bad behavior. Nevertheless, depressed Christians may find it helpful to consider that God has a purpose which depression may serve—like bringing them to "firm ground." It is not merely a capricious event or a shift in their biochemical tides. God is with us not only in the good times but also in our suffering; such grounding charts a purpose for every one of life's events. It can provide meaning for the suffering. I have known counselees who were able, in the midst of despair, to experience God as "ground"—not an enemy but a friend. Others were only able to experience the pain; after the depression subsided, however, many of them came to see it as a "school of suffering," to use Kierkegaard's words (Stone 1996). Still others never managed to reframe their depression theologically.

Unlike cognitive restructuring (chapter 9), which may argue or finesse clients out of their illogical or irrational viewpoints, in reframing the helper adopts the melancholic's perceptions. Counselees, after all, believe their existing frame to be a correct view of reality. Therefore caregivers initially concur with their frame—up to the point of the problem. At that point they assist counselees to begin questioning their frame from within. They find a chink—a lapse of logic, a forgotten or overlooked detail—in the frame's structure. Together they reflect on this chink. The space widens, new light shines on the situation, and change becomes possible.

Depression: A Negative Frame of Experience

It is impossible to pay attention to every piece of information that assails our senses in the course of a day or even a moment. All of our perception is selective. As we choose to frame events positively or negatively, therefore, we are not working with all of the information available to us. Reframing helps depressed individuals to recognize the positive elements of a situation—to see data they have been screening out—and thus to look at events from a more confident and realistic perspective.

Certain events, of course, are more difficult than others to frame positively. They appear to offer little good. (A person who has accepted a new job, moved across the country, and invested an entire life's savings on a house might quite naturally take a dim view of the announcement that the new employer may go out of business.) The perspective must be changed, some positive information must be allowed in—even if one has to work at believing it.

For counselees who have a difficult time believing any positive frame, I sometimes suggest that they *act* for a period of time as if the reframed way of viewing a situation is true. Later we talk about how this new approach has affected their feelings and actions. If they felt or acted more positively, I urge them to continue acting as if the frame is true. Remember that reframing is not the "power of positive thinking" or unrealistic optimism. The positive frame is just as true—or more so—than the negative one, and it is a more humane way of viewing events.

One study of counseling conversations discovered that most counselees—this is certainly true for the depressed—tend to overlook positive changes they have made in their lives, preferring to focus on what is undone (Weiner-Davis, de Shazer, & Gingerich 1987). When helpers focused on past or current instances of positive change, counselees reported increased awareness of other positive changes that they had previously forgotten or ignored. They recalled past situations in which they had solved a difficult problem or ways in which they were presently addressing some difficulty.

A connection exists between reframing and looking for exceptions. When counselees discover ways in which they already have changed for the better or handled challenges in a constructive way, those past successes serve as a platform for the construction of solutions to the present depression (de Shazer, 1985). The purpose of discovering such exceptions is to help counselees frame their depression differently.

Since counselees have a negative way of viewing events, the task of the minister is to promote different perspectives, to help them reframe what is happening in their lives so that hope grows and positive change becomes possible.

Indirect Reframing

Another way to reframe—less straightforward but sometimes more powerful because of its indirectness—is to share the story of a nameless friend (parishioner, counselee) at another time and place who addressed a period of depression successfully. Counseling Beth, for example, who is fearful of offending others, constricted in her behavior, and certain that she has little value on this earth, the minister might relate a story such as this:

I remember a parishioner I knew a number of years ago in California. Her situation was similar to yours in many ways. She thought she was a noth-ing, a contestant for "doormat of the year." She dressed conservatively because she didn't want to stand out in a crowd or give offense. She never ate in restaurants because the food might be too different.

I asked her if she had ever wanted to take a trip to an exotic, faraway place. She said, "Yes, I've always wanted to travel, but I was afraid of all the new and different situations I would have to meet and I didn't think I could handle them. So I've never traveled." I suggested to her, "I would like you to imagine that you're leaving on a trip today. Instead of going to Bangladesh or Brussels, you are going to stay in the same town, live in the same house, and sleep in the same bed. At the same time, like any traveler, I would like you to go and eat in different restaurants, visit places you have never seen, and talk to people you have never met. Also, since travelers do not necessarily wear the same clothes they do at home, I want you to go to a department store and buy some relaxed, comfortable traveling clothes in bright colors and begin wearing them on your trip."

At first she didn't think she would be able to do it. After we talked a little while, she decided to buy one day's worth of new clothes and go to a Chinese restaurant that evening. On some days the following week she did not put on different clothes and visit a new place or eat in a new restau-rant; when she came to see me the following week, she described those days as less enjoyable and more disappointing than those days when she had been on a trip. She liked the idea so much that she kept right on going; the last I heard from her, she was still on her trip. She says the journey is more exciting, more adventurous, more scary, but she is not depressed as before.

I wonder if you would like to take such a trip?

Tell about a person who was very much like the counselee, and who suc-cessfully addressed similar difficulties. Sometimes it makes sense to use a story from Scripture (for example, the woman touching the hem of Jesus' garment). Counselees can discuss what they might do if they were the per-son in the story. In telling the story, help them discover one or several alternative ways of acting or thinking. The goal is to beget hope for a pos-itive future, one that breaks the self-defeating patterns and negative frame of the person's unhappy past.

Establishing Future Goals

Counselees with little hope, according to Lester, "need future stories that provide security, excitement, and joy in the present moment. Pastoral caregivers enable despairing persons to gain the courage to lean into their future, to revision and reconstruct future stories that are connected to hope rather than despair" (1995, 38).

One of the keys to helping the depressed construct new future stories is to help them develop new visions for how their lives might be. Establishing goals is a critical but sometimes difficult task because so many depressed people are frozen in the unchangeable past—to use Kierkegaard's term, their *actuality*—and experience little or no freedom. Goals may not come easily. Persist; do not substitute a form of counseling that only addresses the pastor's interpretation of the problems. From the beginning of the first counseling session, actively assist counselees to formulate a vision for what the future will be like when their depression no longer terrorizes them.

Both pastor and counselee participate in identifying target goals, achievable in a short period of time, and determining how they will reach those goals. (For more information on goal setting in counseling, see my book *Brief Pastoral Counseling*, 1994.) Certainly pastoral caregivers will challenge any goals that are unethical or superfluous to the counselee's situation.

It is especially important for those who are seriously depressed not to try too many changes at once. After the first limited objectives are reached, counselees may wish to establish new goals.

It is also good to remember that the more severely depressed need very small first goals, since pulling out of depression may take considerable time. Missing a seemingly minor goal may cause them to slide deeper into the depression. Pastoral caregivers need patience; working with melancholics can be discouraging—even more so if the methods presented in this book are taken to be panaceas or quick fixes of a complex condition.

I have found two methods especially beneficial in helping people to form goals that express their vision for the future. The first is the *future question*. It can tease out melancholics' embedded eschatology. It goes like this: "How do you want your life to be different one (or three or six) month(s) from now? Be realistic—recognize work, family, and financial constraints—and also be very specific." Possible responses might include: "I will sign up for a computer class so that I can get a better job in the comptroller's office," "I will join Al-Anon and learn how to live with a husband with a drinking problem," or perhaps "I will join the choir at church to help me get out and interact with people."

The *magic question* is another approach. The concept was introduced by de Shazer (1988, 5), who refers to it as the *miracle question*. (I began calling it "magic" after several counselees objected to the word *miracle* as something that only Jesus could do.) The magic question poses: "Suppose that you awaken tomorrow morning and your problem is magically gone. How would you know? If by magic the problem were no longer there, what would be different in your life? How would your family or friends know? How would they say that you had changed? How would I recognize the change?" In later sessions ask more questions, such as: "Are there days when a little bit of the magic has occurred? How are these days different from before?" The secondary questions help counselees realize that change is not only possible but already happening.

A variation of the magic question asks: "Let us suppose Jesus came to you in the middle of the night and told you that when you awoke your depression would be gone. How would you know that it was gone? What would you be doing differently? How would you be thinking differently? How would it change your understanding of God? How would your family or friends know? How would they say that you had changed? How would I recognize the change?"

Any of these approaches facilitates hope by encouraging individuals not only to conceive a new future but also to develop specific objectives that can move them toward that future. Goal-development methods can be discussed in the session and assigned as written homework.

Counseling goals should always be stated in the positive: not "I don't want to be depressed," which focuses on the negative, but something like "I want to return to doing things with my friends whether I feel like it or not." As Berg and Miller (1992, 39) write, paradox ensues "whenever we try to tell ourselves NOT to do something. That is, whenever we tell ourselves NOT to do something we are forced to think about the very activity that we are supposed to avoid." The goal should be a positive one, one that can be achieved in a very short period of time.

The depressed are experts in their problems. When they begin to describe one problem, often others come tumbling out. This snowballing effect is easily misinterpreted as a sign that long-term therapy or referral is necessary. It is also an example of melancholics' negative mindset, which primarily sees what is not done rather than what is done. They need specific concrete goals that they can achieve in a short time. The pastor does best not to allow the counseling process to detour onto problems other than those addressed by the specific target goals—however important they may seem. Simply suggest: "That sounds like something serious. After we have achieved your goal, we can return to it if you would like."

The rationale for leading depressed counselees to choose a specific goal and work solely on that one task is that "change is most likely to ensue from a concentrated focus on a single but significant problem in living (and, conversely, the belief that much natural problem solving is weakened by attempting to deal with too many difficulties simultaneously)" (Wells 1982, 12). Help the counselee who faces an assortment of problems to choose one goal as the highest priority. Since pastoral counseling of the depressed is limited by time, its goals also must be modest. Narrowing the focus to one small goal increases the likelihood that change will occur. Any change at all can lead to hope's return.

Hope-Oriented Conversation

Most people in counseling tend to speak of their problems in the present tense. For the depressed, that present tense represents a negative and even hopeless viewpoint that they assume to be an accurate picture of themselves, their situation, and the world in general. They desperately need to get out of their distorted present. A subtle way to reframe their difficulties is to refer to problems in the past tense, at the same time discussing counseling goals as "when" instead of "if." For example, say "What do you think *will* happen *when* you start to come home earlier from work?" instead of "What do you think *would* happen *if* you started to come home earlier from work?"

Melancholics sometimes describe people close to them in terms of their behavioral flaws. Such descriptions need to be restated. If the counselee claims "My husband is not considerate," restate her claim: "He does not listen to you when you are discussing something." The counseling goal thus changes from sweeping (altering a personality characteristic) to specific (achievable behavioral changes).

For the depressed, one of the biggest obstacles to change is their desire to talk only about their problems; in sessions they often bob and weave away from every initiative to discuss solutions. With such people, ask: "What is the difference between the times when the depression is better and the times when it is worse?" Or use the magic question: Ask "What will be the very first sign that change is on the way?" Most counselees tend to focus on the ultimate answer, when everything will be completely as they wish, and consequently fail to notice the first subtle signs of transition and growth. It is important to raise questions that sensitize them to the early nuances of change.

Some melancholics believe that the problem only resides in someone or something outside of them. They are the victims and blamers. To the minister's various suggestions they will answer, "Yes, *but* . . ." Try to compliment such counselees for their strength despite suffering, telling them you recognize that they still must possess some sense of hope or they would not be there in front of you. Commend them, too, for being good historians of the causes of their problems (Berg 1991). The objective is to change their view of themselves and their thinking about the problem so they can see that they have some part in the solution.

Scaling and coping questions (Berg 1992) are good to use with especially challenging counselees. A *scaling question* might be: "If ten means that you will do *anything whatsoever* to solve the problem of fighting with your wife, and one means that you will just sit there and do nothing, where are you on a scale of one to ten? How about your wife—where would she say you are? Your neighbor? Your best friend? What will it take for you to go from five to six on the scale? What will it take for your wife to say that you have gone from five to six?"

Coping questions can be useful in situations that seem completely hopeless to depressed individuals. "How do you cope? How do you get through the day? How come things are not worse? From what you have told me about your background, how are you coping as well as you are?" Such questions focus on strengths residing within the person that allow them to cope, however poorly.

Strengths

People sometimes mistake what they *see* for what they *believe* about what they are seeing. Most who are depressed believe depression to be their inescapable lot—indeed, their curse—for the rest of their lives. Certain that they are doomed to a life of unending sorrow and pain, they create in their minds a belief system about the hopelessness of their depression. Then they live according to that belief system rather than test its validity.

In reality, I have noted, people rarely are depressed all the time. Even the most severe depression lifts somewhat during portions of some days. The sufferers possess competencies and strengths they do not recognize—or if they do, they pass off the exceptions as false or accidental. I always assume that even those who are depressed come into counseling with many resources. (In a sense, everything discussed in this chapter—reframing, discovering exceptions, and goal-setting—is rooted in the centrality for hope of discovering and building upon people's strengths.) Pastors work out of a unique theological anthropology or understanding of persons, and must help the depressed to believe this different frame and recognize their strengths and abilities rather than focusing on their weakness and pathology. I do not deny the power of sin in people's lives, but I do recognize that melancholic individuals manage their depression better if they recognize and build upon their strengths and allow God to work through them.

Pastoral counseling with the depressed should not break down people's defenses or help them gain insight into their defense mechanisms; neither is needed to manage depression. Instead the pastor builds up or energizes their coping resources and strengths. Educators know that the truest way to facilitate positive self-esteem in children is not to praise, reward, or be nice to them (these are all fine, of course), nor to berate and punish them, but to help them achieve success at their tasks. Similarly, one of the quickest ways to help the depressed feel better about themselves is to entice them to use some of their forgotten strengths. Doing so not only requires less time than breaking down their defenses; it is far more humane. The focus shifts from pathology, problems, and explanations, to competence, strengths, and solutions.

Focus on the *what*, not the *why*, of human problems. Discern which specific behavioral changes will help. Build upon existing skills. When individuals make changes for themselves, they experience relief from the painful stress and demoralization that accompany their problems.

One way to build upon people's strengths is to show them hospitality. The counseling session needs to be a place where counselees are welcomed, encouraged, and complimented for what they are doing well, not where their past wrongs or present pathology is dredged up. Near the end of the initial (and possibly sole) session, and before homework tasks are discussed, it is good to give counselees appropriate compliments. De Shazer writes: "The purpose of the compliments is to build a 'yes set' that helps to get the clients into a frame of mind to accept something new—the therapeutic tasks or directive" (1985, 91). For example: "I'm impressed with how hard you have been working to improve your problem. Even though you have not achieved what you wanted, it is obvious you have given considerable effort to it." Showing hospitality has for centuries been one of the vital tasks of pastoral care.

In a sense the depressed act like pathologists looking for disease. Instead of creating a new vision for the future, they focus on what is going wrong now or has failed in the past. They view the bad things that have happened to them as a predetermined pattern with little chance for positive change. It is tempting for many helpers to concentrate on such counselees' liabilities rather than their strengths or solutions and thus on the past rather than the future. Gilligan (Yapko 1989, 328) holds that "such views advance images of clients as incompetent, sick, or 'broken,' and suggest therapy as a process in which the primary tools for change are the therapist's presumed wisdom and skill. . . . Furthermore, it may organize the intention of both therapist and client around 'errors' rather than 'solutions.'"

A more positive perspective is to think of depression as a sign. Depression is an indication that change is necessary; it is a call for action. Depression does not mean that life is hopeless but that new skills and different strategies for dealing with key areas in people's lives are needed. Remembering and using past skills and abilities are indispensable. Depression ought to serve as a precipitator for new action and redirection in life. This is nothing more than reframing; something that is considered bad (feeling depressed) is given a more positive interpretation (a sign that change is needed).

Depressed individuals are likely to be stuck in the past, to sense little freedom in the present, and to see only a bleak future filled with more suffering. This is a theological as well as emotional plight. Lester comments, "Pastoral theologians and pastoral caregivers, however, are interested in the future dimension for an additional reason—this is where ultimate concern takes us into religious experience with hope and despair" (1995, 149). He points out that counselees' attention to the future, the dimension of hope, includes the "hopeful sacred story in their confrontations with the crises, tragedies, problems, and other life circumstances that they face from day to day." The primary symbol of hope in Christianity is Jesus Christ. Because of his life, death, and resurrection, we have a future hope. Possibilities have opened up to us.

Existence as an authentic self, in Kierkegaard's view, means to look beyond our immediate necessities or past liabilities. It is to anticipate the future with the awareness that we have the freedom—however limited—to actualize whom we ought to become as faithful Christians and to take responsibility for shaping that future. Ministers counseling the depressed need to engender a hope that recognizes the past but also takes action in the present in order to move into that future. Through the use of specific caregiving methods—reframing, recognition of exceptions, establishing goals, using future-oriented conversation, and recognizing strengths—we can help melancholics to create a new future. To act is to recapture hope and thereby to revive faith.

PART
TWO | **Action**

SIX

Brief Pastoral Counseling of Depression: A Fourfold Approach

Nobody knows the troubles I've seen,
Nobody knows but Jesus.

Depression is not the discouragement of a life filled with physical pain, tragedy, or oppression. It is not a short spell of feeling blue, nor is it a passing bout of deep sadness. In fact most normal people—church members included—go through times when they feel down.

Melancholia is different. It affects the total human organism—cognition, physiology, interpersonal relationships, and behavior. Because depression is not a simple phenomenon but one with a legion of causes, degrees, and manifestations, pastors need to tailor their responses to the particular characteristics of each case of depression and the context out of which it arises.

Many people wish to deny their melancholic feelings. They may act strong, in control, upbeat all the time, and refuse to acknowledge their depression. Others may admit to feeling depressed but berate themselves for such feelings, pathologize themselves, see themselves as lazy, good-for-nothing losers and worse; they expect their lives to be like those of absurdly euphoric young adults in beer commercials (so merry they are unable to close their mouths).

Depression does not necessarily mean that something is drastically wrong. Many people experience ebbs and flows in their moods, periods of high and low energy, times when they accomplish a great deal and times when they do little or nothing, procrastinate, and waste time. Life is not like beer commercials. People need to recognize and accept that they can have periods of low mood; the important thing is what they do in response to those feelings.

Neither is depression a mortal sin. It is something that needs to be managed, and melancholics need to develop skills to address it and control it. Helping counselees to understand that they may have a skill deficiency and not a fatal flaw or mortal sin facilitates positive change because, once trained in depression management, they can move forward to a more hopeful and productive future. In fact, that may be exactly why they have come for counseling. Their past and present are miserable. They want a better future, and they do not want it ten or twenty weeks from now.

On average, parishioners who come to their minister for counseling stay for one to three sessions; therefore each pastoral counseling session must focus on key issues, develop a plan for change, and help counselees take concrete action. In other words, each meeting should provide counselees with what they need to resolve their melancholia (Stone 1994) since, for whatever reasons, they may not return.

Assessment of Depression

Let us say that a person who claims to be depressed or exhibits many symptoms of depression has walked into the pastor's office for the first time, asking for help. At the outset, it is important to discern whether the individual is in fact depressed, or has some other configuration of emotions, or possibly a physical illness. Since the traits of depression and its precipitators vary considerably from person to person, the minister must learn the specific ways in which the counselee is experiencing the dysphoria and what might be exacerbating it.

Depression, or melancholia, is known in psychiatric terminology as *major depression* to distinguish it from the normal low periods that many people go through. The psychiatric diagnostic criteria for major depression lists nine symptoms, as follows:

1. Depressed mood, sadness, irritability part of each day, nearly every day
2. Diminished pleasure or interest in daily activities
3. Considerable weight loss or gain, change in appetite
4. Significant change in sleeping patterns (The most common result is early waking.)
5. Marked increase or decrease in movement (Most commonly the person physically slows down.)
6. Fatigue and loss of energy

7. Feelings of worthlessness or guilt (The feelings are beyond the scope of how people would usually feel.)
8. Difficulty in concentration
9. Ideas of suicide or death

To be diagnosed with major depression according to American Psychiatric Association criteria, persons must exhibit at least five symptoms for a minimum of two weeks, *and* have either depressed mood or diminished pleasure or interest on most days for at least part of the day (APA 1994). These criteria are a good basis for determining if someone really is depressed. They certainly are not exhaustive but signal that a person's story may be one of melancholia.

Once depression has been identified, it is necessary to determine the extent or severity of the depression. The extent of a true depression may be ranked as mild, moderate, or severe. In *mild depression,* individuals may feel sad or blue, a feeling that fluctuates considerably. At times, they may feel quite cheerful. Or they may be unaware of feeling especially sad but may lose interest in work or hobbies, or suffer from insomnia or moderate but uncharacteristic fatigue or restlessness. The unwell feeling can be relieved temporarily—or permanently—by outside stimuli such as compliments and jokes, a new job, a vacation, or a piece of good news. Other symptoms of mild depression may be relieved by regular, strenuous exercise, a reevaluation of one's goals, appropriate dietary changes, and so forth.

The *moderately depressed* individual's dysphoria tends to be more pronounced and more persistent, and it is less likely to be influenced by attempts to offer cheer. Immediate relief of this condition usually is temporary, and counseling requires more effort. The depressed mood is frequently at its worst in the morning and may lighten somewhat as the day progresses. Cognitive, physiological, interpersonal, and behavioral symptoms are likewise more resistant to simple solutions. Many such individuals pull away from friends and family, and their relationships may be troubled.

The *severely depressed* live, it seems, on a dismal and barren planet. They are apt to feel relentlessly hopeless and miserable. Those who suffer agitated depression often state that they are beset with worries. In Aaron Beck's study (1967, 17), 70% of severely depressed persons said they were sad all the time and could not snap out of it; they were so sad it was very painful; or they were so sad they could not stand it. Severe depression also is likely to slow people down to an extreme, occlude their thinking process, cause debilitating exhaustion and passivity, and seriously impede their relationships and their normal functioning.

Obviously some depression is so severe that it requires hospitalization. The vast majority of melancholics seen by ministers and other church professionals are only mildly depressed, however, and will benefit from skillful pastoral help. Such pastoral caregiving is not second-class treatment; it is exactly the quality of care needed in such cases. It spreads beyond counseling sessions to include the response of other parishioners, enfolding the depressed into the community of faith.

As a rule of thumb, ministers do best to see mildly and some moderately depressed individuals, referring the more severe cases to pastoral counseling specialists or mental-health professionals. Both minister and congregation, however, still offer support and pastoral visitation to seriously depressed members who are on medications, have periodic psychotherapy, or are in and out of psychiatric hospitals throughout their lifetimes.

A number of standardized inventories of depression can help ascertain the existence and extent of depression. They include the Beck Depression Inventory (1967), the Zung Self-Rating Depression Scale (1965), the Raskin Rating Scale for Depression (1970), and the Hamilton Rating Scale (1969). The Zung Scale is reproduced in the Appendix to this volume. Although the Zung is not the most sophisticated of depression screening devices, it is a solid instrument, simple to use, and it takes little of counselees' time or effort. Using inventories like the Zung is not often necessary, but it proves useful when the minister is uncertain about the severity of the depression—or whether depression even exists.

Depression and Other Disorders

Melancholia often occurs in concert with other conditions. The discussion below describes several disorders that relate to—or masquerade as—depression. It is good to consider them while listening to the counselee's story.

Anxiety. From 10% to 20% of individuals who are depressed also experience panic disorder. Approximately 30% will exhibit symptoms of generalized anxiety disorders sometime during the depression (U.S. Dept. of Health, vol. 1 1993, 47). Some antidepressants can cause symptoms of anxiety as a side effect. Either depression or anxiety may precede the other. Studies of people with anxiety disorders have noted that the longer the anxiety exists, the more likely the subjects are also to be depressed. This has led some researchers to hypothesize that "many persons with concurrent major depressive disorder and panic, social phobic, or generalized anxiety disorders may actually have only a single disorder that presents with both anxiety and depressive symptoms" (ibid., 48).

Eating disorders. One-third to one-half of all individuals with either anorexia or bulimia also experience depression. Indeed somewhere between one-half and three-fourths of people with eating disorders have experienced depression at some time in their lives (ibid., 49).

Obsessive-compulsive disorders. If you think about it, one of the most characteristic activities of the depressed is obsessively ruminating over events of the past. Individuals with obsessive-compulsive disorders are as likely—or more so—to be depressed as those with eating disorders. Indeed, many of the medications authorized by the U.S. Food and Drug Administration for the treatment of depression also help people troubled by obsessive-compulsiveness.

Grief. The minister should remember that grief is not depression—though a grieving individual will usually experience depressive symptoms for a period of time (and inadequate resolution of grief can bring on long-term depression). Chapter 1 described the major differences between depression that is a normal part of grief and significant major depression. Grieving people most frequently describe *bouts* of depression that come and go with decreasing intensity and frequency after a loss, but grieving people who also suffer from melancholia find little relief from their pain for months, years, or even decades.

Medical disorders. Some medical disorders produce depression-like symptoms, such as insomnia, weight loss, and low energy. These medical ailments include endocrinopathies like diabetes; pituitary, adrenal, or thyroid disorders; certain infections; several malignancies; some neurological conditions; collagen disorders; and cardiovascular disease (ibid., 55).

Heart disease. From 40% to 65% of individuals who have experienced a heart attack will suffer depression. Depression following heart surgery is commonplace, yet studies of individuals with heart disease note that their depression is seldom recognized or treated (ibid., 61).

Cancer. Major depression occurs in roughly one-quarter of cancer patients (ibid., 62). Some drugs used in the treatment of cancer cause depressed mood as a side effect. It is noteworthy, however, that the rate of depression among cancer patients is about the same as for individuals with other serious illness.

How Clergy Think about Depression

It is not necessary for ministers to decipher the exact cause of depression—if that is even possible. Many factors influence the onset of depression: genetic predisposition, previous incidence of depression, injustice in our culture, people's expectations and thinking styles, a troubled marriage or dysfunctional family, diet or drugs, and more.

Life is full of tough times. Whenever you apply for a job, you run the risk of not getting it. Whenever you love someone, you risk being rejected when your loved one leaves you or dies. Things do not go as we wish. Besides our joys and accomplishments, we suffer much loss and discouragement. It is not primarily what happens to people that causes depression. Many are turned down for job after job without becoming depressed. Parents die, children get in trouble with the law, siblings commit suicide, spouses leave, houses burn down, businesses fail, but no depression. People have lost entire families in automobile accidents and natural disasters yet, though their grief is unfathomable and will never leave them entirely, do not succumb to clinical depression.

Why, then, do some people plummet into the depths after a tirade from a stranger at an intersection or a perceived snub from a neighbor? It is completely normal to feel bad. How people manage those bad feelings (due in part to their physiology and their past) determines whether they become depressed.

How ministers think about depression is critical, for that shapes how they will treat it. Depression is a *disorder,* not a disease like hypertension. There is no blood test for it. In fact, it may be better to talk about depressions instead of depression since no one variable defines it, as in some other psychiatric diagnostic categories.

When counseling those who are depressed, therefore, it is best to skip explanations such as "fear of failure," "secondary gains," or "codependence." These explanations help neither the ministers doing counseling nor the counselees trying to manage their depression. Pastoral counseling of depression is not a cure. The depressed need to learn or relearn coping skills for managing the difficult times in their lives, and they need to learn how to put those skills into action.

Pastoral Conversation

Pastoral conversation is not dinner-table discourse. It has a clear purpose: helping people to live faithful Christian lives. It assists them in reframing events in order to gain a hopeful, grace-filled perspective on the most troubling situations. It guides people as they wrestle with the ethical decisions necessitated by problems or crises. Pastoral conversation encourages people to accept what they need to accept and to design ways to change what needs to be changed.

If the conversation helps people feel better for a while but does not lead them to see their situation differently or act differently, then it is not pastoral. Even when walking with someone through the valley of the shadow, despair, or intense pain, feeling better is only a side effect of the real goal: to capture a clearer vision of the future, shaped by the Word of God, and to act upon it. To fail to point the way is to bless the sufferer's inaction. To offer emotional support without movement towards a different perspective, a different way of living, is not responsible pastoral conversation.

The wife of an alcoholic, who tells the pastor the details of her husband's most recent drinking bout, takes comfort from a listening ear, but she also needs to learn how to act differently. She needs to become involved in Al-Anon or a similar group and to set clear boundaries with her husband. For the minister to listen without challenging, without pointing the way, may offer momentary solace. But it is a palliative (like aspirin) for the pain she needs to feel—pain that can motivate her to take action, create a life for herself, and challenge her husband with the consequences of his alcohol abuse.

For another illustration: A depressed man in his thirties recites his woes to the pastor. Perhaps he feels better after such conversations, but what he really needs is to see his physician to determine whether he has medical problems that can be treated with medication. He also needs to view events of his life in a more positive way. And, whether he feels like it or not, he needs to act differently—ethically, humanely, and responsibly.

The difference between a *complaint* and *complaining* is that both pastor and parishioner confront and deal with the former. Their conversation calls forth a response, which leads the troubled person to a different view, different actions, and a more sensitized ethical response. Pastors who listen to complaining without spurring people into action fail to take them or their problems seriously.

In distinguishing between complaints and complaining, Beck's comments are useful: "Talking about how miserable and hopeless [counselees] felt and trying to squeeze out anger often seemed to accentuate [their] depression; their acceptance of their debased self-image and pessimism simply increased their sadness, passivity, and self-blame" (1979, 263). Some very well-meaning and loving Christians have invested hours upon hours listening to depressed individuals and running to their beck and call, thereby to an extent perpetuating their depression. To talk with people repeatedly about their depression and listen sympathetically, without urging them toward action, is to offer a stone instead of a loaf.

Melancholics often are so preoccupied with negative thoughts that further introspection tends to aggravate the pervading dysphoria, even if it results in short-term good feelings. In my counseling, the expression of feelings has been effective primarily with acute, but very mild, depression, and then only in the initial stages of care. Hope flowers only when the focus moves from past and present to future. For counseling to have long-term gains, people need to change the way they think and act.

Certain counselees are determined to talk, talk, talk. Since as a rule we err when we keep doing "more of the same" in counseling, it may be useful to redirect the focus of all that talk. Ask about what is not depressing in their lives. Dig a little, urge them to find even the smallest exceptions. Instead of focusing on the depression, these new questions pave the way for constructing solutions out of what they already are doing right, what is going well in their lives.

The First Session

The first meeting with a depressed person needs to cover a lot of ground. Initial tasks include: establishing or deepening a relationship, building rapport, gaining background information on this and previous episodes of depression, and assessing the depression's severity—especially whether the counselee is so severely depressed as to require immediate medical attention or hospitalization.

All of those basic tasks must be done very quickly—if possible, in a matter of minutes—for if hope is not generated early in the first session, the counseling probably will not go well. Remember, *melancholics rarely stay in counseling for many sessions*. Reframing, emphasizing strengths, and setting goals help generate hope. At the outset, communicate that pastor and parishioner are a pair of sleuths investigating the thinking, relationships, behavior, and physical ramifications of the depression. This assessment/investigation is equally the responsibility of the counselee, who in the future will take on the majority of the assessment task. In a collaborative fashion, ask the following questions about the depression to ascertain its severity and to discover what strengths, coping abilities, and possible solutions are available.

1. *The Problem.* What are the immediate difficulties that impede functioning? For example, if the person's marriage is disintegrating, the first intervention may focus in this area. If he or she is suicidal, this must be addressed at once. If there is any possibility of medical problems, referral to a physician is in order. The person may have been laid off, fired, or

passed over for a promotion—a career crisis seems to have precipitated the depression. If so, that is where intervention can begin.

2. *Strengths.* What are this person's strengths? Even melancholics have many skills, abilities, and resources they may have temporarily forgotten or undervalued. These need to be rediscovered and used. Encourage counselees to remember good or successful experiences from the past and to review how they functioned differently in those positive situations.

3. *Characteristics of the Depression.* Are the symptoms primarily behavioral, physiological, cognitive, or interpersonal? Refer to the four symptom areas discussed earlier, and identify a cluster of most-debilitating symptoms to which counseling methods will be directed.

4. *Goals and First Steps.* What are the goals and practical first steps that can be taken to help manage this depression? Both the minister and the parishioner may have a long-range vision for that person's life, but often that is too much to tackle. They need to come up with some realistic objectives or first steps that can stop the slide into deeper depression and initiate the journey out.

Whenever the assessment reveals depression, weigh the suicide risk first of all. If there appears to be a chance of suicide, take appropriate action immediately (for examples, see chapter 3). One does not need to be depressed to threaten, attempt, or commit suicide, but a significant number of depressed individuals do all three. One study found that the suicide rate for depressives is thirty-six times higher than for the general population, and at least three times higher than for either schizophrenics or alcoholics (Beck 1967). Ideas of suicide occur at one time or another in 75% of depressives, and at least 15% make the attempt (Fairchild 1980, 33). Although active church participation is a slight deterrent to suicide in the general population, there is no research to suggest that depressed church members are any less likely to have suicidal thoughts or consider acting upon them.

The assessment process may accomplish a great deal by itself; in fact, certain mildly depressed persons need only to tell their story and set goals. They might not want or need any further visits. (One study comparing interpersonal psychotherapy, cognitive-behavioral therapy, and antidepressant medication discovered that all three methods of treatment significantly helped more severely depressed individuals when compared to a placebo group receiving minimal supportive therapy. It found no significant differences between the treatment groups and the placebo group when the depression was quite mild [Elkin et al. 1989].) It appears that, for some mildly depressed people who are motivated to get beyond their depression, basic supportive care is sufficient to help them weather their melancholy.

If an individual finds more than one visit necessary but is not sufficiently depressed to require referral to a specialist, the minister can follow one of two approaches. One relies primarily on a sustaining relationship "with a twist." During such sustaining sessions, a relatively small specific change is suggested (such as a change of diet, abstinence from caffeine and alcohol, or exercise). It allows for discussing difficulties and imparting some strength to the individual through the minister's presence and support. The pastor also refers such a depressed person to a physician for a physical examination.

If the sustaining course is chosen, it is vitally important to remember the distinction between discussing a complaint and complaining. Supportive pastoral caregiving addresses complaints; it is not for those who come repeatedly to complain but do not want to do anything about their depression. The sustaining course usually sees a person a few (one to three) times, typically widely spaced apart.

The other (from my perspective, typically preferred) option is to begin a process of brief pastoral counseling (usually one to six sessions) that will strive for more significant change on the part of the counselee. To follow this course effectively, the minister will use several of the methods described in the subsequent chapters of this book—methods gleaned from my own practice, from the counseling practice of others in the field, and from research on counseling outcomes.

It may be useful to add that some depressed individuals do not arrive at the church door saying, "Pastor, I feel depressed." They may go to physicians describing back problems or sleeplessness rather than depression; they go to family counselors complaining, "My partner is insensitive to my needs," rather than speaking of their melancholy; they may go to the minister with their guilt or spiritual struggles rather than with an obvious depression. The minister must listen for depression lurking behind somatic complaints, troubled relationships, or spiritual desolation. Although depressed individuals do go to ministers and directly speak of their depression, some melancholics do not speak directly of their pain. In fact, many do not ask for help at all. Friends or family members may tell the minister of this person's trouble. In such circumstances ministers are in a unique position among professional caregivers because they can initiate a visit to the family.

Counseling Methods

Throughout the centuries helpers have used a variety of care and counseling methods to offer help for the depressed; some are still in use today. They include spiritual direction exercises, psychoanalysis, long-term therapy, brief counseling, medications, exercise and diet, vitamins, and more. (We are safely past the era of leeches, alternating hot and cold baths, and incarceration in chains.) Some approaches have put heavy emphasis on exploration of the past in the hope that once people come to terms with their past, they can function better in the present. Others have tried to change how people think on the assumption that more positive, less cognitively distorted thinking will yield less depression. Still others have prescribed marriage and family counseling, assuming that relieving difficulties in these crucial relationships will also relieve the depression. And medications are prescribed for melancholics by practitioners who accept the physiological basis of depression.

Not all counseling methods are created equal, so far as depression is concerned. The U.S. Department of Health and Human Services has carried out exhaustive research on depression for more than thirty years, reviewing various counseling methods and making recommendations concerning their effectiveness. In the clinical practice guidelines prepared for primary-care physicians, they conclude that "The efficacy of long-term psychotherapies for the acute phase treatment of major depressive disorder is not known; therefore, these therapies are not recommended for first-line treatment." They add that counseling which is "time-limited, focused on current problems, and aimed at symptom resolution rather than personality change" is indicated (U.S. Dept. of Health, vol. 2 1993, 4). In a section on treatment indications, they write that "Preferred psychotherapeutic approaches are those shown to benefit patients in research trials, such as interpersonal, cognitive, behavioral, brief dynamic, and marital therapies" (ibid., 37).

We as pastoral caregivers owe those in our care no less than optimal assistance—that is, to guide them to the best help possible and to use counseling approaches that show superior results in current controlled research studies.

Each of the methods presented in the next chapters focuses especially, although not exclusively, on one of the four characteristics of depression (interpersonal, physiological, cognitive, and behavioral). It is generally best to begin by matching change methodologies to symptoms. For example, if a counselee is having marital difficulties, interpersonal approaches would be a good place to start. But it is even better to use several counseling methods, so that more than one of the characteristics of depression is addressed. Change in any one of the symptom areas will naturally bleed over into other areas. A review of research studies on depression indicates that the best treatment sometimes incorporates methods that target more than one symptomatic cluster. Cognitive and behavioral methods, for example, may be used together. In some cases, adding the benefits of antidepressant medications to the treatment plan gives even more effective results, especially with more intransigent depression.

These counseling methods derive from a variety of psychological schools, from the field of pastoral counseling, and from the history of pastoral care and spiritual direction. All, in my experience, have helped depressed persons. A number of them can relieve more than one of depression's four characteristics. Methods that address interpersonal issues, as well as counseling that works to change people's cognitions and behaviors, work about as effectively as antidepressant medications—thus chapters 7 through 10 will focus on interpersonal, physiological, cognitive, and behavioral counseling methods.

The methods presented here and in the chapters to come are in no way complete, and the discussion will of necessity be brief. No minister would ever learn, let alone use, all of them. I suggest that pastors choose methods which seem most appropriate for the people in their care. To be most effective for all their parishioners, they will do well to have a confident grasp of at least two methods for each of the four symptom characteristics of depression—thus equipping themselves to give the best possible guidance and care to all varieties of people in their charge.

SEVEN | Interpersonal Interventions: Strengthening Intimate Relationships

Relationships are like chickens (to paraphrase a famous Woody Allen line): noisy, messy, and hard to control. . . . But we need the eggs. Melancholics, unable to deal with the noise and mess, often don't get any eggs. They can make things even messier for their friends and loved ones, becoming moody and uncommunicative, whining and criticizing, standing up dates and neglecting to return telephone calls. Sometimes they will not smile or answer questions or even say hello. They appear unwilling to make an effort. Indeed, many depressed individuals isolate themselves from everyone around them—both from those who wish them well and those who do not.

Withdrawing from interpersonal relationships is one of the worst things the depressed can do. They may tell themselves, "Nobody wants to be around someone who is down all the time." Some pull away because they are afraid to seem weak or show their feelings. They may surmise that other people could not understand their agony, so they do not ask for help. Many are certain of rejection due to their feelings of worthlessness.

Jay Cleve (1989, 182) states that "loneliness is known to further complicate and aggravate depression. . . . Contact with other people and an ongoing support system are extremely effective defenses against depression." One of the tasks of caregivers is to help the depressed maintain and strengthen relationships with people who can provide them with ongoing support and—after an episode of melancholy has subsided—to develop new relationships as a preventative measure for future episodes. Obviously it is best for the depression-prone to work hard at relationships when they are not depressed. Unfortunately it seldom happens that way, and pastoral caregivers find themselves counseling melancholics who have neglected their relationships or established harmful ones.

Relationships of the Depressed

Several things should be considered when helping melancholics assess their own interpersonal relationships. First, *do not necessarily buy their claims "no one cares for me" or "I don't have any friends."* More often than not, they do have friendships but their negative thoughts cause them to screen out those who care for them or who would like to be more involved in their lives.

Second, depressed individuals must be careful not to rely upon *rescuers.* These are people who want to help so much that they cast about for any wounded strays they can gather in. Rescuers are not looking for a reciprocal relationship in which each person shares and cares for the other. They want a one-way relationship: the rescuer takes care of the poor lamb (the depressed individual). The depressed does nothing but accept the rescuer's attention. The difficulty with rescuer relationships is that they keep melancholics in a passive, dependent posture. They do not allow the depressed to stand on their own feet and act responsibly. This can be particularly prevalent in congregational life. An embedded theology of many Christians in recent years lends itself to this rescuer stance to the degree that it encourages support and caring without any expectations in return. Rescuer theology (gospel without law) that comforts victims is bad theology for the depressed, who need to act independently, ethically, and responsibly. Church members need to learn that discipleship is not solely for helpers; the depressed are called to follow Christ as well.

Third, melancholics need to steer clear of those *hypercritical individuals* whose primary way of dealing with life—including other persons—is to find fault. The depressed tend to be overly critical of themselves already; such friendships only exacerbate the fix they are in. Depressives also tend to be hypersensitive to criticism, so listening to people who are "only telling you this for your own good" can cause the depression to spiral even deeper than before. In fact, fault-finders' criticism often is inaccurate, and the advice they give has a good chance of being very bad advice indeed for the depressed.

Fourth, do encourage melancholic counselees to *tell* significant others about their feelings. Prompt them to express their pain, in small or moderate doses, and to spread out the sharing so that no one person feels overwhelmed. By so doing, the depressed can enlist the help and sustenance of people who probably were not aware of their inner pain—or at least were uncomfortable about bringing it up.

It is difficult and sometimes impossible to convince painfully shy melancholics to pour out their hearts to others. Sometimes they feel freer to express themselves in supportive group situations. Small, existing groups within the congregation (such as a choir or ongoing church school class) or specially created sharing groups are a help for these people. Unfortunately, there are no Powdermilk Biscuits (of Prairie Home Companion fame) to "help shy people get up and do what needs to be done" when they are depressed.

At the opposite extreme are those who burn out family and friends with incessant talk of their sadness, irritation, and anguish. The well-worn counseling directive to "get your feelings out" is counterproductive with such individuals, except in small doses. When sharing with others, typically they invest too much time focusing on the past and on their bad feelings, thus becoming even more depressed. They spend little or no time constructing solutions to their problems. Furthermore, such behavior usually is repellent to friends and relatives who might otherwise serve as a significant support system. These folks need assistance in setting limits on the time they spend expressing their melancholy.

The desperation that comes from feeling emotionally down, powerless, and hopeless can cause the depressed to become very needy. Out of their neediness they occasionally make bad decisions (such as isolating themselves or making friends with rescuers or fault-finders). Pastoral caregivers need to guide these people toward healthful decisions in their interpersonal lives.

Life with a Depressed Person

Not only do family members have to deal with the direct consequences of a loved one's depression; they also need to protect themselves from being swept along the wave of melancholy into their own depressed state. (In this chapter "depressed family member" refers to a spouse, life-partner, parent, child, sibling, or close friend—anyone who is intimately involved with or is inevitably affected by the depressed person.)

Depression is not contagious like the common cold, yet those who live with melancholics for a long time often end up depressed themselves. It is clear that depression does occur more in some families than in others. Genetic causes aside, something akin to burnout results from the exhaustion of living with and relating to a depressed family member.

Life with a melancholic requires enormous resilience of family members; the long-term impact of the depression can fragment the family, causing extensive dysfunction. Therefore the primary task for family members is to *protect themselves* and the family system as best they can. They must learn to live their lives as normally as possible. If a wife is exhausted from the stress of looking after a depressed husband, she becomes a candidate for depression herself. When that happens, there is no one in the family to care for either one of them. If they have children, the difficulty multiplies.

Knowing about depression does not lessen the pain that family members experience from the short temper, the neglect, the emotional distance. What should they do about it? Recognize it, be honest about it, and get some kind of counseling or support. Melancholics are not irritable or hard to live with on purpose; they do not have it in for their loved ones. The former stigma concerning depression has been shrinking fast in recent years, and family members of the depressed generally are willing to talk about it. If they do not tell you (the pastor) directly, they will tell someone, and word will get back. You are involved.

When a Family Suspects One of Its Members Is Depressed

Clergy who encounter depressed individuals in their congregations often are in a position to give care to the families as well. Indeed many times it is a family member who contacts the minister first. Often family members do not know how to proceed; they need practical advice about specific actions they can take.

Has Mother been staying in bed all day? Does Dad wake at 4 A.M. and prowl the house? Does he snap at the children for no good reason? What about Grandfather's recent low mood and little jokes about suicide? Sister's plunging grades and quick tears? When families suspect that one member is depressed, their pastor can help them with the task of assessment. A psychiatrist is not necessarily needed for this assignment. Direct them to write down in detail the specific behaviors, relative to typical characteristics of depression, that they can observe. Instruct the family to look carefully for any recent changes in behavior.

If depression seems to be a possibility, their next task is to get the person to the family physician for a complete physical examination (and to a psychiatrist, if it seems indicated). Sometimes one family member needs to accompany the troubled individual to the doctor's office, or at least help prepare a list of specific feelings and behaviors, so that the physician will have complete and accurate information in the brief time that may be given to the examination. Even though some physicians have little expertise in counseling depression, they can determine if there are any physical causes for the behavioral changes, and they can prescribe antidepressant medications. (It is worthwhile for ministers to find HMO hotline numbers as well as a few physicians who are experienced in the treatment of depression.)

Sometimes people who are depressed do not want to admit their depression and refuse to see a physician (let alone a minister or counselor). In this situation family members are advised to make advance preparations—compiling names and telephone numbers of physicians as well as counselors or psychiatrists—so that when the depressed lowers her defenses and agree to see someone, they can act *immediately.* "Immediately" means making the telephone call at once, and seeing a physician or counselor the same day or in the worst case no more than forty-eight hours later. This may be inconvenient or difficult, but depressed persons' openness to consulting doctors or counselors often lasts for a very short period of time.

As a rule, when people are first diagnosed with depression the physician will prescribe antidepressant medication. For the family this is a critical time. Many people who begin a regime of antidepressants stop taking the pills soon after they have started. They do not like the side effects—the lethargic, dulled feeling that some people experience during the first few weeks, the upset stomach, or other annoying reactions. Often—no matter what the doctor tells them—they think of antidepressants as drugs like aspirin or Valium: If I am depressed, I take it; if I feel fine, I do not. (As described in the detailed discussion of antidepressants in chapter 8, these medications work in an entirely different way.)

When individuals are taking drugs for their depression, family members should do everything possible to keep them on the medications for at least a month or two. It is best not to fight with them, just bring the pills at the appointed time. Often the administration of antidepressants is one family member's assigned task during the first month. After three to four weeks, if the medications do not seem to be having an effect or if the side effects remain problematic, depressed individuals should return to the physician to have their prescriptions reviewed and adjusted.

Another critical phase for the family occurs when the depressed start feeling better; a large percentage of them want to stop taking the medications, but family members must do everything possible to ensure that they continue taking them. In an all-too-familiar scenario, a melancholic stops taking medications for a day or two and announces "I still feel fine" or even "I feel better." Just as antidepressants have a cumulative effect and take a month or several weeks to reach their optimal level, they do not *stop* working after four or even twenty-four hours. The person will continue feeling well for a period of time after stopping because of the residual effects of the medication.

After several days, when they start feeling depressed again or family members convince them to restart their medication, they probably will feel worse. The residual effect of the medication has worn off somewhat; it may take another one to four weeks for the medication's effects to return to optimal levels—and what is worse, the side effects often return as well. At this point the depressed may stop taking the antidepressants altogether. This is a time of increased risk of suicide; after feeling better, perhaps almost normal, they are plunged back into despair that is now compounded by the renewed side effects of the drugs.

Early recovery due to medication is no time for the family to return to its usual life as if the depression did not occur. Family members do not instantly recover from its impact. Depression creates problems in relationships, and they will need to address the consequences of what was said and done during the depression. Counseling for the whole family is very important at this stage, because it can treat the depression's impact upon the family. The melancholia has been handled medically; now the family has to address the interpersonal fallout. They also need to work together on planning how to respond if the depression should return.

Individual versus Couple and Family Counseling

Even though it is (and may always be) unclear whether depression causes or is caused by problems in relationships, research data supports the use of couple and family counseling in cases of depression. "In a comparison of interpersonal psychotherapy with and without involvement of the spouse, the two approaches reduce depressive symptoms equally, but interpersonal psychotherapy with the addition of the spouse was more effective in improving marital satisfaction" (U.S. Dept. of Health, vol. 2 1993, 79). Therefore, whenever there is a depressed person and a troubled marriage, marriage counseling should be a preferred method of responding to the depression. The depression does not have to be treated first; it is best to deal with both at the same time. In fact, counseling the troubled marriage or family *is*, in truth, caring for the depression. Research studies reveal that marriage counseling in such situations is superior to other forms of intervention (ibid., 80).

This is not to say that marriage and family counseling is the only way depression should be treated. Pastoral caregivers need a multifaceted approach to depression (which is itself multifaceted). Interpersonal problems in families often occur with depression. One study indicated that there is a direct relationship between common descriptions of marital discord and the symptoms people describe during depression (Beach, Sandeen, & O'Leary 1990, 66). "Feeling discouraged about the future, feeling that one is being punished, feeling disappointed in oneself, and experiencing loss of interest in significant others occur both in depression and in marital discord uncomplicated by depression." Certainly, spouses in a troubled relationship have a head start toward becoming melancholic if these symptoms of marital discord continue for a time. If either spouse is physiologically vulnerable to melancholia, ongoing marital discord can bloom into depression.

Couple and family counseling addresses the distressed relationships as well as the depression. Since depression tends to be a recurring disorder, treating an acute depressive episode with the couple or family not only deals with their immediate distress; it helps protect them from (and prepare them for) potential future episodes of depression.

Couple and Family Counseling

There is nothing especially distinct about couple and family counseling with a depressed family member; pastoral caregivers employ the same methods they would use with families where there is no depression, and they require the same skills in working with systems. Nevertheless, in these situations ministers need to consider a few added factors that are specific to depression. The rest of this chapter examines skills and information needed to address these special concerns: joining, reframing, affirming strengths, helping the family get accurate information about depression, responding to divorce or the threat of divorce, limiting the symptoms of the depression from dominating the family, avoiding the "cheer up" syndrome, handling power differences in depression-plagued marriages, and teaching social skills. (Note that most of the discussion focuses on couple counseling but applies to family counseling as well.)

Joining

Ministers must decide in advance how they will *join* the family, how they will establish or deepen their relationship with all of the family members. Do not become a rescuer! It is easy for pastoral caregivers to get overly involved and do more for the depressed than is necessary—or, when the depressed person does not respond to the help tendered, become irritated and pull away. Clergy need to intervene with expertise—in an adult, rather than paternalistic, way.

Do not side with the depressed, especially when they are acting like passive victims. Recognize the frustrations and difficulties of the nondepressed partners as well. Compliment them for their caretaking. Even their moments of frustration and anger communicate that they care for the melancholic partner. Pastors can take over some of those caretaking activities; this transferring of responsibility gives nondepressed partners a vacation from the weight of caregiving for a brief period, and allows them to see the relationship in a more positive light. It also allows the depressed to exercise more initiative and self-caring. Although appreciated in one sense, the caring and tending of family members can become oppressive to the depressed, who have little energy to struggle against it.

Frequently the process of joining is best accomplished by talking with spouses separately for part of the first session. When doing this, see the couple for an hour and a half, spending ten to fifteen minutes with each and then working with them together for the rest of the session. (Any subsequent sessions are the typical one-hour periods with both spouses present.)

Reframing

In *reframing* the depression more positively for both spouses (see chapters 5 and 9), one helpful reinterpretation is that depression serves a purpose for the relationship by signaling that there are issues that need to be addressed. Another is simply to provide accurate information about depression to family members, which allows a more neutral than negative frame (see Getting Accurate Information, page 84). Information about the typical progression of a depressive episode is especially helpful. Point out that depression will abate with time; it is not a permanent condition. Explaining the cognitive worldview of depressives also helps family members to understand that, although depressed persons may express feelings in a certain way, those are their *depressed feelings* and not their "true" feelings. While they are depressed, people view the world and other people differently. Sometimes reframing depression as a condition with a biological/genetic basis can help family members to avoid personalizing the symptoms. Whatever the approach, a new frame needs to be adopted and shared by both partners.

Affirming Strengths

Since depressed people (and frequently their spouses and family members) develop negative viewpoints about whatever is happening in their relationships, the minister is wise to shift the focus to their strengths. Work vigorously to accomplish this task. Take care not to allow the family to dwell predominantly on the past or to concentrate on problems. Once they recognize their strengths realistically, families can use them to begin resolving their problems.

Getting Accurate Information

Family members need accurate knowledge about depression. A discussion of depression and how it affects people in all four areas of experience—behavior, cognition, interpersonal relationships, and physiology—is critical. Sometimes family members think that they are the cause of a person's depression. The pastor should be especially careful to see that children have not drawn this conclusion. During an information-giving session, provide data on local resources where family members can find answers to their questions. Suggest (or give them) helpful pamphlets or books. Urge the couple to ask questions of their physician or psychiatrist. Some communities have support groups for the depressed and their families and these also can be useful. World Wide Web sites can offer information and support (see the epilogue for a list of possible community and Internet resources). Asking questions and gaining information can help the family view the depression in a less negative light.

Responding to Threats of Divorce

Incidence of divorce or threats of divorce is greater in relationships with a depressed spouse. Even if neither spouse mentions divorce in the counseling session it most likely is hovering nearby. Raise the issue. The depressed may consider it because they envision no hope in the marriage and see divorce as the only solution. Spouses may contemplate divorce as a result of the frustrations of living with depression for years; they are getting little from the relationship and may be tired of trying. Let them know that these thoughts are common, but also that they are by-products of the depression. This is not to indicate that their marital problems are insignificant but to underline the tremendous impact that depression can have on marriages and families.

Limiting the Effect of the Depression's Symptoms

When one parent is an alcoholic, it is almost routine for a family to tailor all its activities in response to the parent's drinking. The same occurs in a family with a depressed member. Everything revolves around the depressive's moods and there is no normal family life. It is vital, therefore, to ensure that melancholic symptoms do not dominate the family. This does not mean that the family should try to strip all control away from the depressed person, only that they not allow the depression virtually to control the family. To this end, encourage families to review everyday functions and determine ways in which these tasks can be carried out with as little disruption as possible from the melancholia. For example, a family decides to take a trip to Florida at Christmastime. At the last minute, the depressed mother does not feel like going. With their pastor's support, the family goes ahead with the trip, providing care for Mom back home. Not only is this healthy for the father and children; the mother's depression loses its power to control the family.

Family meetings are a useful way to ensure normal family life—or at least a semblance of normal family life. Suggest that couples or families meet weekly to discuss the basic tasks of living and communicate openly about important issues; it is a valuable first step to breaking depression's hold on a system. In these meetings they can set clear boundaries that will minimize melancholia's influence over their well-being.

Avoiding the "Cheer Up" Syndrome

It is impossible to argue people out of their depression. Melancholics hear, sometimes day after day: "Cheer up." "Look at the bright side." "Things will get better." Some people even quote Scripture: "All things work together for good for those who love the Lord." It has not worked, it does not work, and it will not work. As a pastoral caregiver, stay out of this trap, and make sure family and friends do the same. If people want to be depressed, let them. If they say they want to stop being depressed, then use methods of counseling that will facilitate their managing the depression.

Remember the basic rule of thumb never to do "more of the same" in pastoral counseling. If it hasn't worked in the past, why do it now? Family members and friends have failed to argue melancholics out of their depression for hundreds, perhaps thousands of years. It is time to do something different (Stone 1994).

Negotiating Power Differences in Marriage

Depression affects the balance of power in couple relationships. Since depression is more common among women, these paragraphs will focus on marriage counseling when the depressed individual is the wife. It applies to depressed husbands as well.

Melancholics are deficient in psychic and physical energy. This, added to the male-skewed power structure of society, makes it especially difficult for a depressed wife to raise issues in the marriage and negotiate her power. It may result in the negation of her feelings and rights in the relationship. Indeed the husband may, in a well-meaning effort to care for his wife, take over some of her daily responsibilities and make decisions for her, thus compounding the effect of powerlessness.

The balance of power between husband and wife is an especially important issue in marriage counseling when one individual is depressed. In the short run, confronting power imbalances in the relationship can sometimes make things even more difficult, but in the long run it is necessary to protect against future recurrence of depression—or at least against its debilitating effects.

Teaching Social Skills

People who have been depressed on and off for an extended period of time need to learn, or relearn, specific social skills. Research indicates that the depressed tend to seek out fewer social events and interpersonal contacts than nondepressed individuals, initiate fewer contacts with new acquaintances, and perform less capably in interpersonal and social interchanges. Melancholics describe themselves as less comfortable in social situations, often sensitive to being ignored or rejected, yet lacking social skills that are indispensable for easy acceptance. They also may lack ability to be assertive. It falls to the minister, in counseling depressed individuals and their families, to help them develop assertiveness, learn whatever social skills they lack, and use those skills to improve and increase their relationships.

Such social training may be done in many ways; the pastor's approach is up to his or her own experience and creativity. Methods that have been helpful for me include the following:

1. Model methods of social interaction for counselees.
2. Role-play specific social events that are especially troublesome to the depressed.
3. Give instructions on some of the niceties that are required in social occasions.

4. Teach assertiveness training.
5. Encourage the person to join a church group that is especially sup-
    portive, empathetic, and open to new members. (Be aware that some
    church groups are closed and unreceptive to new people, especially if
    the new members are somewhat reclusive and depressed, or even
    "odd.") Sometimes it is helpful to contact one especially helpful,
    empathetic person who will smooth the counselee's entrance into the
    group.

Communication

Sometimes it seems that melancholics have two styles of communication:
nonexistent and bad. In marriages with a depressed spouse, studies have
found that communication between partners was quite inhibited—inter-
rupted episodically by verbal fights with expression of negative emotions,
followed by a continuation of the inhibited communication and emotional withdrawal (see Prince & Jacobson 1995 for a review of studies).
Problem solving between the husband and wife was rarely constructive, if
even attempted. The angry outbursts led to feelings of helplessness and
hopelessness—major characteristics of depression—in at least one, if not
both, of the partners.

Both partners need to find ways to communicate more effectively. A
depressive's irritability and negative point of view have an impact on how
the couple communicates. Interpret this to the nondepressed spouse as
well as to the depressed spouse. Sometimes pastoral counseling may focus
principally on helping them to communicate positively with each other.
Since depression in a family frequently leads people to pull away from each
other, reestablishing aboveboard positive communication is a major step
toward dealing with the depression in the family system.

Couples and families with at least one depressed member show less
bonding and less companionship. They do fewer pleasant things together.
They are distant from each other and feel isolated. Strong marriages value
companionship; thus one of the early tasks of marriage counseling is to
help couples structure times when they can communicate with each other
in a positive nonthreatening way.

Effective communication helps to break the isolation and strengthen
the bond between partners. It is best to begin by scheduling brief sharing
sessions for couples. Initially, these sessions cover nothing more than
telling one another how their day has gone—no comments, no criticisms.
Later sharing sessions can expand the topics of conversation. Only after the

couple is able to communicate effectively about neutral events in their lives are they to address specific problems in the relationship. Even then, it is usually best to do this first in a counseling session—after which the caregiver asks, "How can you mutually solve this problem?"

Problem Solving and Change

Coyne (1986) believes that depression among the married is at least partially caused by the couple's ineffective coping with marital and family difficulties. Improved communication will raise the issues and may provide a vehicle for resolution, but ultimately it is not sufficient unless it leads to problem solving (Clinebell 1984; O'Hanlon & Weiner-Davis 1989; Stone 1994). In cases of depression, couples need to learn and use more effective problem-solving skills. Coyne (1986, 498–99) puts it this way:

> It is neither depression nor depressing circumstances, but the couple's problem-maintaining solutions that are the focus of the treatment. . . . Change comes about when (depressed individuals) are provided with an experience that shifts their point of view or framing of the situation. . . . Preparing the couple to act differently is therefore given priority over the development of insight or the exploration of feelings.

At the beginning, it is easier to switch what depressed individuals are doing to something more constructive than it is to move them from passivity to activity. Work at negotiating small changes in a few problems of the relationship. This is essential because both partners need to experience success in their efforts. The nondepressed spouses typically believe that they have given all they can give to the relationship; they feel drained and unwilling or unable to give any more to it. Do not push for major efforts or sweeping changes in the relationship, but negotiate very small, specific changes that can be accomplished in a week. The time period needs to be short, and the changes small but significant for the relationship. When the first negotiations lead to success, larger changes and more major issues can be addressed.

Even though the depressed usually are isolated and deficient in interpersonal skills, melancholia never attacks one person at a time. For those who are married, the malignant feelings and behaviors spread to partners and children as well. Pastoral caregivers are in an ideal position to aid all members of the system, whom they may already know through church activities. After urgent issues are addressed when the depression first comes to light, the best approach is to do couple and family counseling. In this way, the melancholic will return home to an environment where people understand what is going on, are able to cooperate, and participate in the process of change. Families thereby protect themselves from depression's fallout and guard against recurrent episodes in the future. It is important to remember that the entire family system has suffered, perhaps for years; through improved communication and effective problem-solving skills the family can recover and face a more positive future together.

EIGHT | # Physiological Interventions: Prozac and Beyond

Smash your thumb while pounding a nail. Not only will you feel pain in your thumb (or even your hand and arm), but you will feel light-headed and your knees may wobble. The body is a system, and it functions as a unit. Any change in one part has an impact on the other parts.

Although no one knows the extent to which physiology affects depression, few would deny that it does. Forty years ago, depression largely was considered a psychological disorder. Today, depression's biological constituent is widely acknowledged.

Depression occurs in some families more than it does in others. If one parent has a history of depression, the children are more likely than the general population to experience depression. When two parents have a history of depression, the children's chances are even greater. Twin studies have further revealed the physiological aspects of depression; identical twins separated at birth have been studied at length in order to separate genetic causes from the effects of environment. Such studies have found that if one twin experiences depression, the other is likely to become depressed as well, even though they have been raised in different family environments (DeBattista & Schatzberg 1995).

Further evidence of the physiological causes of depression was discovered recently, when it was reported that the left side of the prefrontal cortex—the part of the brain necessary for processing emotions—was smaller in depressed people than in a control group (Damasio 1997). Although the findings on the prefrontal cortex need to be replicated, clearly there is a growing body of literature that suggests a significant physiological basis for melancholia. In fact, some forms of depression appear almost solely biological in origin.

Unfortunately, the minister has few care-giving methods available to cope with physiological symptoms. Medications are the obvious treatment method. But the world of antidepressant medications is confusing; there are so many of them, with so many different dosages, side effects, and interactions with other drugs, that pastors often (understandably) simply leave the medications to the doctor. Since pastoral caregivers are likely to have conversations with families or physicians about their parishioners, and need to understand a drug's side effects as they counsel the depressed, this chapter will provide a basic description of the different types of psychotropic drugs. It will cover what they do, how they work, their side effects, and when they should not be used. Read it, then save it as a reference for the future when you encounter a counselee who is taking a particular antidepressant. For the latest information on antidepressant medications, the World Wide Web can be an excellent resource. (See the epilogue.)

Physiological Vulnerability

An acquaintance of mine was visiting an old high school friend when, to her embarrassment, the friend's son loudly announced, "You're much thinner than my mom!" She quickly replied, "Well, yes, God made our bodies all different, and it's a good thing. It would be pretty boring if we all looked alike."

Not only do our bodies look different; they respond differently to similar events. When stressed, one person's neck tightens up, while another gets tension headaches, colitis, ulcers, insomnia, or high blood pressure. Some individuals seem more vulnerable to stressors; their bodies are racked by anxiety while others sail serenely through equally difficult situations.

Just as some people appear to be wired for anxiety, it seems that some are similarly wired for depression. They are especially susceptible to any potentially depressing episode, however slight—while others can experience tragedy, loss, failure, or humiliation, yet suffer only mild grief or passing sadness.

Linda, a past counselee of mine, wanted a new living room couch for the mobile home she and her husband rented. She had saved money for months to buy one when, out of the blue, her husband brought home a new Harley Davidson motorcycle with a high-interest, five-year payment plan. Most people would become angry, complain about the cost of the Harley, or use it as an excuse to go ahead and buy the sofa on credit, but for Linda it was the beginning of a downward spiral into severe depression.

I saw her through several depressive episodes thereafter, each one activated, if there was an observable cause at all, by a seemingly trivial event. Nathan Kline states that depression "is probably triggered by some disarray in the biochemical tides" (De Rosis & Pellegrina 1976, 208). It is my sense that certain people, like Linda, are more physiologically susceptible to these biochemical tides than others. In effect they are more sensitive to events or stressors that may precipitate depressive symptoms; they have a preexisting physiological vulnerability to depression.

Research seems to confirm a chemical/genetic/physiological basis for at least some depression. Although it may be comforting to know that there is a biological link to depression, it can also become a way of rationalizing irresponsible behavior. I have seen counselees rest in this knowledge to such an extent that they refuse to make any changes in the way they live their lives. They act as if they are totally predetermined, moved only by the onrushing biochemical current. Their bumper stickers might read: "Nothing can be done, therefore I will do nothing." It is vital for counselees—whether or not their depression is physiologically based—to work at making changes in their attitude, thinking, behavior, and interpersonal relations so that they will not be debilitated by present or future episodes of depression and so the impact upon their families, friends, and coworkers can be minimized.

Body Image

Standing in the grocery checkout line, our eyes scan racks of magazines picturing lithe young women and trim, muscular men on the covers. They are the "ideal" images packaged and sold by the advertising, fashion, and entertainment industries—and internalized by many people. Standing before a full-length mirror, few can measure up. Although the purpose of this book is not to help men and women to cherish their own bodies, ministers must be aware that body image can be a significant issue. People need to value their bodies, to accept them realistically, and to resist comparing them to magazine covers.

Over the years I have counseled a number of depressed individuals who had poor body images and viewed themselves as fat. Several approaches have proved helpful. First I urge them to become more active. They choose some physical activity in which they can have fun and achieve a degree of success. It can be anything—bicycle riding, dancing, running, walking, swimming, racquet sports, aerobics classes, working out at the gym, or gardening. If, after becoming physically active, they still want to do something more about their weight, I usually suggest groups such as Overeaters Anonymous or Weight Watchers, depending on the nature of their overeating. I do not recommend an immediate weight-loss effort for the depressed because the majority of people who lose weight gain it back again. Weight loss is better undertaken in a more positive mood, after other depression-related issues are addressed.

Illness and Medications

A wide variety of ailments can cause fatigue and other depression-like symptoms. These can include influenza, cancer, asthma, chronic fatigue syndrome, severe allergies, migraine headaches, heart disease, malaria, infection, brain tumors, and many, many more. Some physical illness may be so exhausting that the person feels unable to do anything more than very basic tasks, and therefore may be misdiagnosed as depression. Hypothyroidism can cause depression-like symptoms, as can Cushing's Disease. General medical diseases or events (heart attack, heart surgery, stroke) may also bring on depression, or at least depression-like symptoms.

Medications sometimes can precipitate or exacerbate depression. Some of those who come to the pastor with depression may be seeing several physicians for various complaints and obtaining medications from each of them. Unfortunately, such people often fail to tell every physician what else they are taking, and may use up to a dozen different drugs that may well be interacting with each other. In such situations, the caregiver should send them to one of their doctors who will take inventory of their prescriptions, evaluate the total constellation of medications, be in contact with the other physicians, and determine if there are any inter-drug reactions.

Some prescribed medications can cause depression as a side effect: drugs such as some antihypertensives for high blood pressure, including reserpine, methyldopa, hydralazine, propranolol; and anti-Parkinson's medications such as levodopa and bromocriptine. If depression is triggered by a drug, the physician ordinarily can find another one which will not produce that side effect—or can decide whether the benefits of a particular drug are being eclipsed by the side effect of depression.

Depression is complicated in some cases by the use of readily available drugs, most commonly alcohol and caffeine. Alcohol is a depressant and, though possibly giving some short-term relief, will only heighten the melancholy (see chapter 1). I customarily urge depressed counselees to abstain from alcohol totally or trim down to a couple of drinks each week—and never to drink alcohol when they are feeling especially down.

This also goes for illicit drugs such as barbiturates and marijuana. Caffeine found in coffee, tea, many soft drinks, chocolate, and diet pills seems to affect depression in some people. It gives a momentary high followed by a greater down. Even sugar, in excess, will act as a drug, causing overstimulation of the pancreas and resulting in higher insulin output, thus causing low blood-sugar levels, irritability, and possibly depression-like symptoms.

A number of melancholics have their most difficult period in the morning. Many routinely begin their day with several cups of coffee, toast, and a glass of orange juice (which is surprisingly high in simple sugar). At midmorning they may add two or three more cups of coffee or a cola and a doughnut or Danish pastry. So, in the five hours or more after the deprivation of food during sleep, they have ingested primarily sugar and caffeine. A few people can trim wide mood swings in the morning simply by beginning the day with at least twenty grams of protein; no doughnuts, sweet rolls, or other sugars; and no caffeine beverages.

Diet change alone will not help the majority of individuals who are depressed. For one recent counselee, though, these changes and the addition of regular exercise were enough to bring about significant change in the depression, and only one counseling session was needed. The counselee did not have any exceptional situational precipitators for his depression—outside of the normal stresses and strains of his life—but he was in need of some physiological changes.

Hormones

Hormones may precipitate or exacerbate depression. A few depressed individuals have abnormalities of the hypothalamic-pituitary-adrenal, hypothalamic-pituitary-thyroid, or growth hormone secretions (Potter et al. 1991, 635). Some researchers have associated depression and the menstrual cycle, though the degree of relationship varies from study to study (DeBattista & Schatzberg 1995). Other studies have failed to establish a conclusive relationship between the two. Natalie Shaines (De Rosis & Pellegrina 1976) notes in her research that women in the premenstrual phase have greater feelings of irritability, anxiety, and helplessness. Catherine Dalton discovered that half of women who commit suicide do so in the premenstrual or first four menstrual days of their cycle. Judith Bardwick noted that the premenstrual time is one of anxiety. She hypothesizes that progesterone and estrogen may have an influence on the central nervous system, which has an impact upon the monoamine oxidase levels, which are associated with depression. She also suggests that when women experience the high estrogen time of their menstrual cycle, they are less likely to experience depression (ibid.).

Even though research has not established a direct link between menstrual cycle and depression, women can test whether there is a relationship for themselves by charting their menstrual cycles, moods, and behavior for two or three months. If there appear to be times during the cycle when they experience more depressive symptoms, they can prepare themselves for those low periods and refrain from blaming themselves or others for what may be a hormonal event. They can also see their physician to determine whether hormonal supplements would benefit them.

Medications for Depression

The human brain is a complex electrical system of nerve cells. It works by sending electrical impulses that carry information from one nerve cell *(neuron)* to another and control the systems of the body. In essence, it enables communication between neurons by releasing chemicals *(neurotransmitters)* into the space between the two cells, known as the *synapse*. Neurotransmitters move from one neuron to another via the synapse. They are received at the second neuron through *receptors*—specific places on the neuron where the neurotransmitter can be received.

The brain has several types of neurotransmitters. The monoamine neurotransmitters (serotonin, norepinephrine, and dopamine), which carry messages about thinking and feeling, are linked to depression. A person is susceptible to depression when any of the monoamine neurotransmitters is deficient or there is a problem with the receptors in the neuron.

Antidepressant medications are designed to alter the balance of neurotransmitters at receptors. They increase the availability of neurotransmitters so that the neurons operate optimally (DeBattista & Schatzberg 1995). After they have relayed the message from one neuron to the other, the neurotransmitters break down so that new electrical impulses can be transmitted across the synapse. Some antidepressant drugs slow that process, on the assumption that depression is less likely to exist if sufficient monoamine neurotransmitters are present. Several recent drugs hinder the tendency of some monoamines to return to the neuron they originally came from (reuptake inhibitors).

Here is another way of looking at it. Imagine that the brain is a large archipelago. For cargo to get from one island to another, it needs a boat or ferry. So a system of ferries carries goods between islands. The islands are neurons, the waters in between the islands are synapses, the cargo is needed information, and the ferries are the neurotransmitters. More ferries mean that more cargo can travel from island to island; one kind of antidepressant medication focuses on making more neurotransmitters, or ferries, available.

Sometimes the ferries malfunction; they make a U-turn before reaching their destination and return to the home island. This tendency to return to home port is called "re-uptake." The solution is to close the home port. Medicines that block re-uptake prevent the cargo from returning home so it can arrive at its destination and deliver the message.

The archipelago metaphor is a simplified view of how antidepressants work. Of course they do not work exactly the same way for all people. We all have heard tales of our friends' and family members' experiences with antidepressants. A few are horror stories, but more often than not they are miracle stories. Knowledge about the more commonly prescribed antidepressants will allow ministers to converse easily with people experiencing depression and also to have some understanding of the potential biological and behavioral effects of these medications. We are certainly not physicians and do not prescribe drugs; nevertheless, an understanding of some of the more common antidepressant medications and how they work will make our pastoral caregiving more effective.

In a previous work (Stone & Clements 1991) I encouraged the use of medications for treating depression. My views have not changed; indeed, with the recent development of antidepressant medications that have fewer side effects, I would endorse the use of antidepressant medications with even more enthusiasm. Because they primarily treat the physiological element of depression, they work in concert with counseling methods that address the other three components: cognition, behavior, and interpersonal relationships.

The U.S. Public Health Service especially recommends a combination of medications and counseling in three instances. First, both are useful when either medication or counseling alone is not fully beneficial. Second, parallel methods are appropriate when it appears that both medications to address symptoms and counseling to address psychological causes of the depression are needed. Finally, the person who is chronically depressed or has had poor success with either one or the other method of treatment in the past is a candidate for therapy that combines drugs and counseling (U.S. Dept. of Health, vol. 2 1993, 26).

Many counselees think antidepressants act quickly like aspirin or Valium, but in fact they function in an entirely different way. Aspirin reaches its peak efficiency in about thirty minutes and wears off in about four hours. It takes ten days to four weeks for antidepressant medications to achieve their intended effect, and some theorists have suggested it may be two months before the drug makes its full impact. Indeed, some researchers believe that it may take this long to create the necessary changes in the receptors of the neurons (DeBattista and Schatzberg 1995). When the drugs are discontinued, it takes weeks for their residual effects to disappear—thus a person who says "I stopped taking my pills and I feel better" may be correct, temporarily, because the side effects of the medication are reduced while the residual effects of the drug are still at work. But in time the effects of the medication will wear off and the depression is likely to resume.

If an individual does not respond well to one antidepressant drug, there is a good chance that another may be more suitable. Therefore, ministers do well to urge depressed parishioners to take their antidepressant medication faithfully as prescribed, but if side effects continue to cause problems or there are no positive effects after four weeks at proper dose, to talk with their physician about switching medications—not abandoning them.

Types of Antidepressant Medication

Several types of antidepressant medications are used by physicians to alleviate depression. They include tricyclics, monoamine oxidase inhibitors (MAOIs), selective serotonin re-uptake inhibitors (SSRIs), and other new medications.

Antidepressants have been used for over four decades. The *monoamine oxidase inhibitors* were the first in use (iproniazid was introduced in 1956). MAOIs include phenelzine (Nardil), tranylcypromine (Parnate), and selegiline (Deprenyl). They are effective as antidepressants, but because of possible serious drug interactions and other side effects (individuals taking MAOIs have to follow a special diet), they are the least prescribed of all antidepressant drugs today. Pharmaceutical companies are working toward a new generation of MAOIs that will have fewer side effects, but until then few if any of the people ministers encounter in counseling will be using MAOIs.

Tricyclic medications are the second category of antidepressant drugs. Imipramine (Tofranil) was first used in 1958, and since that time a number of tricyclic medications have been developed. Common trade names for these drugs are Asendin, Elavil, Norpramin, Pamelor, Sinequan, Vivactyl, and others. Until the introduction of Prozac in 1988, tricyclics were the standard in the treatment of depression. Patients do not have to follow a specific diet, and there is little danger of lethal drug interactions. Nevertheless, some physicians have been reticent to prescribe tricyclic drugs, especially with highly depressed, suicidal individuals, because of the ease of overdosing. In addition, some people on tricyclic drugs stop using them because of uncomfortable side effects. Elderly individuals and those on high dosages are liable to experience dry mouth, blurred vision, weight gain, sedation, difficulty in thinking, urinary retention, constipation, orthostasis, and even sometimes arrhythmia. Sedation is one of the most common side effects, therefore tricyclic drugs are best taken at bedtime. For most people, the side effects of tricyclic medication decrease over time.

Recently several new antidepressant medications have revolutionized the pharmacological care of the depressed. *Selective serotonin re-uptake inhibitors* (SSRIs) are now the primary medications used for depression. Prozac, the first of several SSRIs, was introduced in 1988. Since that time millions of individuals have used Prozac—so much so that it has become a subject of jokes and talk-show conversation. The new drugs are popular because they work as well as or better than MAOIs and tricyclics and have fewer side effects. They are also difficult to overdose on and therefore safer to prescribe to suicidal individuals. As a result, the new drugs have allowed relief for melancholics who could not take earlier antidepressant medications because of possible drug interactions, potential for suicide, or unpleasant side effects. SSRIs work by hindering the return (re-uptake) of neurotransmitters like serotonin to the neuron they originally came from.

Selective serotonin re-uptake inhibitors are increasingly being prescribed for obsessive-compulsive disorder, eating disorders, anxiety disorders, and some chronic pain conditions as well; higher doses of SSRIs are needed for treating obsessive-compulsive and eating disorders than for depression and anxiety. Although they have fewer side effects than earlier drugs, they sometimes cause temporary gastrointestinal upset, which is reported by between 20% and 40% of all individuals on SSRIs. But most indicate that the side effects decrease over time—or they learn to live with them. Taking SSRIs with meals can lessen stomach upset. Other possible side effects of SSRIs are insomnia, restlessness, and sexual difficulties (DeBattista & Schatzberg 1995).

Prozac is perhaps the most commonly prescribed antidepressant drug. Dosages are usually around 20 mg, but vary from 5 to 80 mg. Side effects are gastrointestinal problems, headache, insomnia, sedation or its opposite, and difficulties in sexual performance. Serious side effects are extremely rare. One reason for the widespread use of Prozac is that it works *and* its side effects are minor compared to those of the previous monoamine oxidase inhibitors or the tricyclic drugs. The several word-of-mouth reports that Prozac caused obsessive suicidal or homicidal thoughts or actions were largely anecdotal and have not been supported by large controlled clinical studies (Potter, Rudorfer, & Manji 1991).

Paxil (Paroxetine) is another SSRI with few side effects. Paxil is sedating for some individuals and is therefore useful for those who are anxious as well as depressed. Still other individuals find Paxil activating. Zoloft is an SSRI with side effects similar to Prozac, but it is less likely to cause insomnia. Another selective serotonin re-uptake inhibitor is Luvox. Dosage ranges from 50–300 mg, with 150 mg considered a typical dosage. Luvox is FDA-approved for the treatment of obsessive-compulsive disorder as well as depression. Individuals on other medications have to be careful about taking Luvox because of possible drug interactions.

Wellbutrin is another recent antidepressant medication. It is not a selective serotonin re-uptake inhibitor and does not have sexual performance side effects like some of the other SSRIs. It is not sedating. Trazodone, around since 1981, has seen a recent increase in use. It hinders the re-uptake of serotonin like the SSRIs, but chemically it works in a different way. Trazodone is quite sedating and useful for individuals who also struggle with insomnia or anxiety, although some physicians consider it not to be as good an antidepressant as some of the more recent SSRIs. Men should carefully discuss taking Trazodone with their physicians since there are rare reports of its causing priapism—prolonged erections that may require surgical intervention.

Serzone is an SSRI useful for depressed individuals who are also anxious or have difficulty sleeping. It was largely developed to be an improved, second-generation Trazodone with fewer of the side effects typical to SSRIs, but it must be used carefully with some other medications, such as antihistamines. Effexor has the same results as the SSRIs listed above. Potential side effects are elevated blood pressure or tremors. Effexor not only hinders the re-uptake of serotonin but also the re-uptake of another neurotransmitter, norepinephrine.

Another entirely different drug, lithium carbonate, has had good results with some severely depressed individuals with bipolar disorder. A salt that occurs naturally in the blood, lithium was first used for the treatment of the manic phase or "high" in the mood swings of manic-depressives. Research is still under way to determine its benefits for major depression. It is sometimes used at low dosages along with tricyclic medications and is reported to help more than 50% of individuals who at first are not helped by tricyclic drugs or monoamine oxidase inhibitors alone (Potter, Rudorfer, & Manji 1991).

Pastoral Caregiving and Antidepressant Medications

Peter Breggin and Ginger Breggin, who are somewhat critical of the use of medications for the treatment of depression, believe that such drugs give people a message that they lack the "psychological or spiritual resources to triumph over [their] depression" (1994, 200). Popping a pill to address spiritual desolation or taking medications to soothe *Anfechtungen* certainly would avoid facing one's spiritual struggles or wrestling with one's faith. But the spiritual side of human beings is not separate from the physical side. If a medication were available to ease severe back pain without making someone fuzzy-headed, it would make sense to use it—even if the severe pain could potentially be an avenue for deepening in the faith. If medications can help one to greet the day, to be more faithful followers of the Christ, to be more responsible in the day-to-day ministry to which each of us is called, then it seems to me that such medications are worthwhile. Drugs are no way to escape our demons, but they may help us meet our demons with clearer heads and lighter hearts.

Although it is not the minister's task to determine whether medication is indicated, the following are several considerations for referring a depressed parishioner to a primary-care physician or psychiatrist for assessing the exigency of antidepressants.

Once again, individuals who are seriously suicidal require immediate attention, and referral to a psychiatrist or primary-care provider is critical. (Chapter 3 discusses how to assess suicide risk and deal with suicidal counselees.) Those who have recurring, severe episodes of depression should also see a physician to determine whether medications may be of use. Since recurring depression is hard on the family as well, family members need as much assistance as possible to limit the spreading impact of a series of depressive episodes.

Severe melancholia is another indication for referral. People who are deeply depressed typically cannot be helped adequately by parish pastors— nor by psychotherapists, who cannot legally prescribe drugs. Medication can give severely depressed persons enough psychic energy to begin performing the tasks that counseling requires. Depressed individuals with significant problems in the workplace also ought to be referred for possible medication (see the research of Sotsky 1991).

Ministers do well to establish referral relationships with local psychiatrists and primary-care physicians who are especially knowledgeable concerning antidepressant medications. (Eighty percent of physicians prescribing antidepressants today are primary-care physicians, not psychiatrists.) It is important to choose a physician who can communicate effectively with both patient and pastor. Less than half of primary-care physicians treating depressed people spent three or more minutes discussing it with them, a 1993 Rand Corporation study determined (Cowley 1994, 42). This raises the concern that physicians, perhaps because of their busy schedules, may move too quickly to medications and ignore other issues in the lives of their patients. Most critics of the Prozac generation are not opposed to the drugs per se, but to the use of antidepressants as a shortcut, avoiding important lifestyle issues that need to be examined and changed. Certainly the zero-to-three minutes of time given by half of the physicians in the Rand study is not enough to cover those concerns.

No one antidepressant medication is clearly superior to another. There is not one drug that benefits all individuals, but there is evidence that if one medication does not work, another will (U.S. Dept. of Health, vol. 2 1993, 55). Ministers should urge parishioners to talk to their physician about prescribing alternative antidepressant medication if the first one has debilitating side effects or does not provide relief after a suitable period of time.

A major drawback of antidepressants has nothing to do with the drugs themselves; it is the tendency of depressed people to take their pills erratically or stop taking them altogether. Several studies on patient compliance with prescribed medications have found the rate of compliance to be about 50% (ibid., 25). Although many ministers do not want to be in the position of pushing medications, I believe it is wise to urge depressed counselees to give their medications time to work, to take them as prescribed, and to keep on taking them if they are helping.

Many people do not want to be dependent on drugs, yet outcome studies of antidepressant medications indicate that drug therapy is highly successful. Parishioners need to understand that anti-drug sentiment is appropriate for illicit drugs, but that antidepressants are in an entirely different class. They also need to understand that taking their medication erratically will increase the possibility of unpleasant side effects and minimize or eradicate the drug's benefits. Here the pastor, like any good educator, might ask counselees to explain the medication's functioning in their own words. We cannot assume that all physicians are making these important points clear to their depressed patients—or that the patients are hearing them. Generally it is recommended that people stay on their medications for four to nine months after their depressive symptoms have receded (ibid., 5).

Since some of the recent antidepressants are more expensive than the older tricyclic antidepressants, a few health maintenance organizations (HMOs) have limited their use in an effort to control costs. The minister who encounters people with significant side effects, or who have stopped taking their tricyclic drug because of its unpleasant effects, might suggest that they talk with their primary-care physicians about one of the more recent medications and find out if the physician will advocate with the HMO for its use.

Most HMOs have determined that drugs are less expensive than psychotherapy and as a result encourage pharmacological treatment rather than counseling. There is a reason that physicians are so widely prescribing Ritalin for children with attention deficit disorder and Prozac for depressed adults: They work *and* HMOs consider them to be cost-effective (which is not always a valid assumption). This is both good news and bad news. The new drugs may become more available, but managed-care companies may also limit the amount of psychotherapy or even pay psychiatrists more per hour for managing patients with medications than with psychotherapy (Pollock 1995, A1).

It is interesting to note that the drug industry recently has spent millions of dollars a year advertising antidepressant drugs. It has paid off. Between 1994 and 1995 the number of prescriptions for antidepressants doubled, and in 1995 doctors wrote 36 million prescriptions for antidepressant medications (Yapko 1996).

I believe in the appropriate use of antidepressant medications and have seen them work wonders in people's lives. I would not hesitate to take them if needed. Still, ministers do well to remain suspicious about the unbridled use of pharmaceuticals, and especially of any drug billed to fulfill what seems to be the American image of happiness. The line between taking medications to address a physiological deficiency, and taking them to achieve the contemporary notion of happiness that permeates so much of our culture, is perilously blurry. When I consider that distorted image portrayed daily in the media, I remember the centrality of suffering and the importance of spiritual struggles and desolation in the life of the Christian (see chapter 2). We may recommend and even endorse antidepressants, but not blindly, because we as a people are on the verge of seeking a pill for every problem, a feel-good potion to erase the pain inherent in living. No need to struggle through the dark night of the soul, no need to face and overcome suffering.

When drugs are the exclusive form of treatment, there is a better than 50% chance of relapse. The relapse rate after psychotherapy alone is lower (Antonuccio, Danton, & DeNelsky 1995; Hollon, DeRubeis, & Seligman 1992). Remember that approximately one-third of all depressed people are not helped by or cannot take antidepressant drugs. In addition, some individuals resist taking *any* drugs or do not tolerate the side effects of antidepressants. For these people, counseling is the only option.

The choice is not simply therapy or drugs. Some depression clearly is physiologically based; other cases are not. Much of the time we simply do not know the degree to which any particular case of depression is caused by physiology, interpersonal relationships, behavior, or cognition. Even if the depression is biologically originated, that does not mean that it must be treated by biological means. The advantage of counseling is that it can help people learn how to manage their depression. It is as effective as medication. It offers built-in relapse prevention in that it teaches people how to think and act differently so that future episodes of depression are less likely to occur.

Sleep Disturbances

Loss of desire for food or sex may accompany depression, but seldom do the depressed seem bothered by it—at least not enough to ask for help. A physiological symptom that *is* of great concern to many melancholics is sleep disturbance, and it is experienced by a majority of mildly, moderately, and severely depressed individuals. Such difficulties may consist of early morning waking, difficulty in falling asleep, or the kind of restless sleep from which people awaken feeling as if they never really slept. Disrupted sleep patterns are especially troublesome for melancholics because long-term sleep deprivation can cause confusion, fuzzy thinking, daytime sleeping, irritability, fits of anger, nervousness, and other symptoms that may seriously exacerbate the depression. Most people will regain their typical sleeping patterns after the depression has lifted. In the meantime, the minister can offer a number of suggestions to help them sleep better:

1. It is important that they use the bed (if possible, the bedroom) only for sleep and sex. It is not a good idea for people with sleep disturbance to watch television, read for long periods of time, or study, in bed.

2. If they are not sleepy, they should not stay in bed. When depressed people lie awake in bed, they may obsessively rehearse their negative thoughts. It is far better for them to get up and do something constructive. The occasional loss of a night's sleep is not harmful and may help them sleep better the next night.
3. Explain to depressed individuals that they actually get more sleep than they think. Many who believe they were lying awake all night actually slept a good deal, but part of their negative thinking is to believe they are unable to sleep.
4. Help them to become active during the day. People who spend most of the day sitting, watching television or surfing the Internet, and taking naps are disinclined to sleep at night. It is better to be as physically active as possible and not take naps.
5. Regular exercise can be very helpful, except in the last two hours before sleep, because it can serve to stimulate and energize as well as relax.
6. A fixed bedtime routine can cue people that it is time to sleep. One such routine might begin with a warm bath before watching the nightly news, followed by a period of quiet meditation and prayer, followed by eating a high-carbohydrate snack, possibly with some protein. Emphasize that anyone with sleeping problems should always avoid stimulants such as tea, coffee, chocolate, caffeinated sodas, and so forth, especially prior to going to bed.
7. Use relaxation methods. Frequently (though not always), learning to relax physiologically also causes the mind to slow down, and obsessive negative thoughts quiet down as well. Some relaxation cassette tapes can be very helpful in this task. (Other methods that address obsessive thoughts, discussed in chapter 9, may also be of use.)

Exercise

A final physiological method is exercise—especially cardiovascular exercise. Long before running was in vogue, researchers found that people who performed regular cardiovascular exercise (at least three times a week) had less depression and less anxiety than did those who were sedentary; and they slept better.

Some depressed individuals want to go from being couch potatoes to becoming Florence Griffith Joyner in a week. They set themselves up for failure. A physical examination by a medical doctor is a good first step; a mild exercise program can follow. One difficulty with exercise is convincing counselees to do it regularly. Try to help the depressed person find exercise activities that bring enjoyment as well as cardiovascular benefits. They do not have to be traditional sports! For example, they might get a dog and take the dog for daily walks.

Exercise is beneficial in several ways. It obviously helps people to stay physically fit and thus stronger and more energetic, and it offers a sense of accomplishment. Here is something they can do. It introduces some discipline into what is often a haphazard life. Discipline gives a sense of self-control to depressed individuals who tend to feel they have no control over anything. Anything active—country and western dancing, cleaning house vigorously, even picking up trash along the highway—also can serve as a distraction from obsessive negative thinking and shift their focus to positive thoughts.

The physiological basis of depression is known and well-documented. Pastoral caregivers, whose primary tool for helping the depressed is conversation, cannot prescribe medications but should have an understanding of their uses and side effects in order to participate fully with doctors and others in caring for their depressed parishioners. The new breed of antidepressant drugs are effective and have minimal side effects for most people, but studies have shown that in most cases of mild or moderate depression, brief and solution-based counseling methods work about as well. Providing counselees with strategies for getting more sleep and more exercise will often give them the clear thinking and vitality needed to help bring their depression under control. People who are physiologically vulnerable to depression may never completely escape its influence, but they can learn skills to manage it, to move confidently into a better and more responsible way of living, and to serve others.

NINE | **Cognitive Interventions: Changing How People Think**

You are what you eat, it has been said, and there is a kernel of truth to that. And when it comes to depression, you are, to some extent, what you think.

People who are depressed seem to undergo a shift in their cognitive mental organization. Negative thoughts begin to dominate, and misconceptions develop, because of faulty information-processing. Melancholics experience disturbance in three major thought patterns; they view events, self, and the future pessimistically—what Beck calls the "primary triad" (1967, 255–61). It seems perpetual. They conceive of their interactions with the world as defeat, disparagement, abandonment, and deprivation; they perceive neutral or even positive transactions with other people as failures. Cognitively, they hold themselves in lower esteem during depressive episodes than when they are not depressed.

Typically melancholics also experience God and their faith in the same negative and hopeless manner. Although religion is not based on cognition alone, the depressed tend to be especially troubled by doubts, see God as distant or angry, and may lose their faith entirely.

Most of the distorted thinking that plagues depressives occurs in microseconds. These "automatic thoughts" (Beck 1979) occur spontaneously while they are going through (or recalling going through) critical events in their lives. Things are happening fast; they need to respond, to make decisions. In such situations there is no time to assess or collect data. One's response is based on these microsecond automatic thoughts that include tacit assumptions and habitual ways of attributing meaning. The automatic thoughts of the depressed often are distorted, illogical, even irrational.

Misinterpreting Experience

Theorists examining the cognitive components of depression describe six ways in which melancholics cognitively misinterpret their experience of events, themselves, and the future in a negative way (Beck 1979; Burns 1980):

1. *Arbitrary inference.* The depressed draw inferences about experience that are counter to or in absence of supportive evidence. The golfer who tells himself, "I'm a rotten golfer and the guys are only tolerating me; I know they're going to dump me as soon as they find someone else for the foursome" is drawing an arbitrary inference, for in fact his golfing buddies enjoy playing with him and give him no reason to think otherwise.

2. *Selective abstraction.* The depressed focus on one minor detail while ignoring the more crucial features of a situation, then view the whole situation based on this one detail. For example, during an otherwise perfect physical examination, Maria's doctor casually mentions a new but harmless mole on her shoulder. Certain she has melanoma, Maria falls into a paroxysm of melancholia and prepares to die.

Discussing selective abstraction in spiritual direction, John Loftus (1983, 219) points out that "It frequently happens that a person simply cannot acknowledge the forgiveness and love of God because he/she cannot move beyond the details of sinfulness." They fasten on one detail of their sinfulness and refuse to look beyond what they have done to what God has done.

3. *Overgeneralization.* As the term indicates, depressives can draw conclusions about themselves, their worth, and their ability to perform from a few isolated incidents. An athlete suffering from depression overgeneralizes if he goes through a slump, then concludes that his career is over, the fans hate him, he's "a bad father and a no-good bum." Melancholics in the midst of spiritual desolations assume that they will continue unendingly.

4. *Magnification and minimization.* In the midst of depression, people do not perceive events accurately. They tend to blow small, negative occurrences out of proportion, and render almost insignificant their positive accomplishments. During a performance review, Julie's supervisor mentions in an offhand way that this company prefers its employees to dress more formally than Julie is accustomed to doing. Because she is struggling with depression, Julie cannot even hear the many positive comments from her supervisor; she assumes she is a failure and about to be fired because of her "shoddy" appearance. Minimization works in the opposite way but with much the same result. When they view their strengths, they deprecate them or overlook what they do well.

Being faithful to the call of Christ requires careful and honest self-reflection, and serious examination of faults as well as strengths. Depressed individuals with a tendency to magnification or minimization, however, do not take a realistic assessment of themselves; they magnify their faults and minimize their strengths.

5. *Personalization.* The depressed may take responsibility for adverse external events when there is little or no basis for such a connection. Fernando and his family lose their house and everything they own in a Gulf Coast hurricane. Fernando falls into a deep depression and blames himself for their losses because he did not accept a job offer in San Antonio years before. Clearly he is personalizing the disaster and taking responsibility for events far beyond his control. (Personalization is a dangerous cognitive distortion for pastoral caregivers as well; when their counselees do not get better, they assume blame for what they ultimately could not control.)

6. *"Either/or" thinking.* The absolutist, dichotomous thinking of depressives categorizes all that they do in one of two opposite positions: perfect or defective, all or none, immaculate or filthy, and so forth. Since depressives can never fit the "good" (perfect) category, they see themselves as "bad" (defective).

It is not hard to imagine what the depressed can do with the passage from Matt. 5:48: "You, therefore, must be perfect as your heavenly Father is perfect." In attempting to be perfect they fail miserably and spiral into deeper depression, lacking a realistic sense of the gray areas in which most of our lives are lived. Melancholics who engage in either/or thinking frequently assume that if they are unacceptable by their own estimation, God cannot accept them either.

Few depressives are pessimistic about everything, but most tend to be sensitive to certain triggers that set their negative thinking in motion. Most cognitive theorists believe that childhood experiences serve as the basis for the formation of negative beliefs about oneself, the future, and the external world. These negative concepts or cognitions may be latent, but they come to life as a result of some specific external precipitator that has dynamics similar to those negative childhood experiences. Even though it is true that past experiences can lead depressives to misinterpret events, however, it is not necessary to explore the past to bring about change. In fact, depressed individuals already spend altogether too much time thinking about the past and not enough time functioning in the present or planning and working for the future.

Information-Processing Errors

Sometimes melancholics' cognitive distortions are so subtle that others (including their pastors) are taken in by them. To prevent this from happening, ministers need to be aware of the common ways in which depressed individuals cognitively misinterpret experience. Such information-processing errors can manifest themselves in concrete thinking, emotional reasoning, misplaced concreteness, and the depressed's response to guilt. Thus the depressed mentally skew what is happening around them but firmly believe their perceptions to be accurate.

Concrete Thinking

Often the depressed look for specific, concrete objects of blame for their distress. Garrett's romance breaks up, and he exclaims, "Women!" He does not see the multitude of factors that contribute to a failed relationship, such as work pressures, circumstance, family, friends, his own behavior, and, yes, *one* particular woman.

Sierra, when asked why she has come for help, replies, "Bosses are all alike. My supervisor is making my life miserable—he's out to get me, just like the others." This is concrete thinking. (It turns out that she had problems under her previous supervisors as well, and may need to look at her own responses to authority.) The task of pastoral caregivers is to help counselees understand the context, to discern (for example) that different people in authority act in different ways, or that not all women treat their lovers badly.

When counseling depressed individuals, caregivers sometimes have to spell out every step needed to resolve their depression. Abstract suggestions ("Communicate more with your wife") do not help. The minister should describe in detail that conversation—what they will talk about as well as when, where, and how. Role-playing such conversation can help; modeling it may be even better. The problem is that when depressives are missing information, they fill in the holes with what they believe (their negatively biased thinking).

Emotional Reasoning

Emotional reasoning occurs when people allow their feelings to dictate their behavior (Burns 1980). They assume their thoughts are accurate because they *feel* accurate. "I feel (that I cannot do anything right), therefore I am (incompetent)." Feelings cannot be relied upon as accurate tests of reality. "Go with your feelings" was a popular sentiment of the 1960s, but it is a terrible thing for depressed individuals to do. A task of the pastoral caregiver is to convince them *not* to go with their feelings.

Those offering spiritual care, writes Loftus, need to be warned that "taking emotions as the sole criterion for truth is as dangerous spiritually as it can be psychologically (1983, 215). Thoughts, actions, and, most importantly, directions toward or away from God must also be evaluated in an integrated and comprehensive way."

Misplaced Concreteness

The logical fallacy of misplaced concreteness, notes the philosopher Alfred North Whitehead (cited in Bateson 1987), occurs when people believe that the name for something and the thing itself are identical. The depressed and those who counsel them must be careful not to regard the construct "depression" as equivalent to "teddy bear," "elk," or "espresso maker." *Depression* and *teddy bear* are different constructs. One is an idea, ephemeral and hard to define, while the other is a concrete object. Yet many melancholics hold on to their depression as tenaciously as a two-year-old holds on to a stuffed toy; to them it is tangible and very real.

Guilt

Scripture speaks of guilt for sins against God and others. The depressed, many of whom are tormented by feeling guilty, do not differentiate between being guilty and feeling shame or guilt. They are self-blamers. What is more, little of their guilty feelings involve the breaking of moral precepts. According to Jay Cleve, the guilt feelings that most influence depression "accompany self-criticalness, over-responsibility, and hypersensitivity to the disapproval of others" (1989, 79). Depressives—who already feel bad—begin to believe their words of self-disparagement. Bad feelings lead to thinking of oneself as bad, which leads to believing oneself to be guilty. And the deeper their bad feelings about themselves, the more likely they are to expect even higher standards for themselves. It becomes a vicious downward spiral.

Feelings of shame and guilt are meaningful emotions for a few seconds or minutes, when they serve as a red flag that something *may* be wrong. Beyond that, they are worse than worthless. Guilt feelings arise not only because of a realistic sense that we have transgressed against God or neighbor but also because we do not make the bed the way our mothers did or we do not have an interest in automobiles as our fathers had.

Guilt feelings need to be examined realistically in order to judge if they are based in moral reality. If a real transgression has occurred, then it is our task to address the wrong, make amends, change behavior, and seek for-giveness. A person who has offended Mother by making the bed less per-fectly than she does (or not making it at all!) needs to let it go, turn a deaf ear to that inner critical voice, and move forward. Guilt feelings that do not subside, but actually increase over time, lead to resentment and sap already-depleted energy needed to manage the depression. Guilt feelings alert us to possible wrongdoing, but serve no purpose after we have listened to them.

Changing How the Depressed Think

When people stubbornly persist in their negative thinking, despite evi-dence to the contrary and the urgings of their family and friends, it is tempting to throw up one's hands. "He refuses to change. What can I do?" You can lead a mare to water, it seems, but you cannot make her drink. But in truth, counseling interventions *can* change negative thinking and teach a new set of reality-based beliefs. Arnold Lazarus (Beck 1979, 9) believes that "the bulk of psychotherapeutic endeavors may be said to center around correction of misconceptions" that either precede or follow actual change in behavior.

Of course it is not easy to change another's cognitions. Ministers, trained in pastoral care and counseling as well as theology and philo-sophy, are probably the best equipped of all helping professionals to enable people to change their beliefs. After all, much of ministry, not just pastoral care, strives for such change.

Cognitive restructuring is a term for the process of helping persons to see the world more realistically and to change unfounded beliefs, mis-interpretations, misconceptions, and expectations. The church has gen-erally acknowledged (although post-1950s pastoral counseling practice often has not) that our beliefs about the future, self, others, the world, and God greatly affect how we act. Cognitive psychological theorists rec-ognize this as well, but they state it in other terms.

One study indicated that cognitive restructuring using religious themes alleviated symptoms of depression more effectively than did classic pastoral counseling, which failed to emphasize changes in thinking (Propst et al. 1992). Cognitive restructuring, the method of changing beliefs out-lined below, is one I have described elsewhere in greater detail (Stone 1994). It includes the following steps:

1. *Assessment.* One of the first tasks of pastoral caregivers (and of coun-selees) is to discover the core negative assumptions or misconceived beliefs that the depressed hold about themselves, others, God, and the world.

Arbitrary abstraction, emotional reasoning, either/or thinking, and the like first must be discovered.

2. *Teaching/Learning*. The next task is to help depressed individuals change their erroneous beliefs. Exposing cognitive misconceptions is the easy part of the process; relearning is much more difficult. Explaining to the depressed how people do faulty information-processing or develop irrational beliefs can help them learn the ways they negatively distort their own thinking (discussed above).

3. *Practicing*. The third step is the movement from *learning* about negative misconceptions, to *catching* them when they occur. Depressed counselees need to recognize their own irrational thoughts and reformulate them in more reality-based ways. If they are doing emotional reasoning, for example, they have to recognize and replace it. They have to find accurate information about their misinterpretations and then replace the distorted thinking with thinking that is more congruent with reality.

Depressed counselees may not catch their cognitive misconceptions right away—sometimes not for several days. When they are suddenly overcome with a wave of depression, the caregiver should urge them to stop and mentally move backwards to discover the trigger of the depression (if one can be discovered) and identify their automatic unrealistic thoughts and beliefs. Again, it is vital not only to discover unrealistic thoughts and beliefs but also to replace them with thinking that is realistic. Their goal is to believe the new reality-based thoughts (or at least act as if they believe them).

Vicky was deeply depressed when she visited me several years ago. She complained that she had failed miserably in raising her daughter, going on and on about how she should have spent more time with Michelle when she was growing up and less on her own career. By the time she walked into my office she had given herself quite an emotional flogging. Her inner critic had the upper hand, and she was miserably depressed.

When the torrent of self-accusation subsided for a moment, I asked, "What has brought you here *now?*" After a new wave of self-attack she revealed that, although Michelle had been accepted to several good colleges, she was turned down by the school of her choice.

Vicky distorted her thinking in several ways. With *selective abstraction* she focused on one small detail and ignored all she had done for her daughter (Michelle herself had recovered from her disappointment by the time Vicky came to see me). She *overgeneralized,* drawing conclusions about her self-worth from one incident. *Magnification* occurred when she blew one relatively unimportant incident out of proportion. She also *personal-*

ized her thinking, taking responsibility for something that happened only to her daughter.

Once Vicky was willing to evaluate her cognitive distortions, she rapidly constructed more reality-based thinking and worked at catching her habit of blaming everything that went wrong in her daughter's life on herself. She challenged her old way of thinking and considered the limitations of her control. Her depression and hand-wringing diminished, and she gained energy to do the things she wanted to do.

Sometimes encouraging counselees to image difficult situations in their minds before actually facing them in real life helps them recognize how they distort cognitions. In *cognitive rehearsal,* counselees picture themselves going through all of the steps involved in a certain activity (such as a mother talking with her daughter about colleges). They then discuss with the caregiver the specific roadblocks and potential conflicts that might arise while actually doing the activity. They report all their irrational thoughts and attempt to correct these cognitive misconceptions on the spot. They are urged to pay attention to every detail and then to work out strategies for carrying out the activity in real life. They imagine the activity several more times to discover further cognitive misconceptions and to begin feeling comfortable with the step-by-step process required for carrying out the act. Ministers need to be aware that individuals who are quite depressed may have difficulty concentrating and their minds may wander. They need your patience and gentle urging.

Countering Rumination

Often the depressed ruminate about events in their lives. From their first waking hour until they go to sleep, whenever there is a free moment, their minds return to their obsessive thoughts—musing, pondering, mulling, hashing and rehashing the same notions over and over again. Several counseling interventions can help such people control their obsessive thoughts. They include thought stopping; write, read, and burn; worry time; and yellow tablet analysis.

Thought Stopping

It is impossible to think of two very different things at the same time. Based on this principle, thought stopping is a mode of relief for individuals who are unable to dispel their obsessive, ruminative thoughts. After explaining the procedure, the pastoral caregiver urges counselees to sit back, close their eyes, and relax. They then think of and visualize an image that poses no threat—for example sitting in their living room and reading the newspaper—and indicate by raising their left index finger that the image is fully developed. Immediately, the pastor yells "Stop!" They do this three or four more times and then possibly repeat the procedure with other innocuous images. Once counselees feel comfortable with the method, they bring to mind their most common obsessive thought and indicate it by raising their left index finger. Again the pastor yells "Stop!"

For one moment at least, the obsessive thought is banished by the shout, "Stop!" After each presentation, the caregiver asks if the thought has disappeared, if only for a short time. When it has, the caregiver responds, "Good. Each time you practice this, you will become better at dispelling your unwanted thoughts."

After a number of exchanges in which the pastoral caregiver yells *stop*, counselees are asked to bring to mind the obsessive thought and shout *stop* themselves. After they are proficient at that and report dispelling the unwanted thought, they are instructed to do it mentally, without saying anything out loud. In repeated exercises they alternate between saying *stop* and thinking it. Eventually they became comfortable and assured at doing it either way. Finally, when they are able momentarily to dispel the obsessive thought at will, they are instructed to do it only subvocally.

Two homework assignments can enhance success in thought stopping: first, counselees practice it for five minutes three times a day, purposely bringing obsessive thoughts to mind and then banishing them with the thought-stopping procedure. Second, they use thought stopping every time they find themselves obsessing about something.

Counselees will not always report at the next session that everything went well. Sometimes they have difficulty setting time aside to practice thought stopping or believing in its efficacy. Thought stopping seems magical, and most people do not believe in magic. Instead of abandoning the method, it is best to repeat much of the previous session in order to reinforce it. See if there are any questions. Again urge counselees to practice thought stopping, and tell a story or two about others (without using names or recognizable details) who have used it successfully. Thought stopping is usually more beneficial when used with other counseling interventions.

Write, Read, and Burn

Divorce, in my experience, is one of the most common subjects of ruminative thoughts among the depressed. They cannot stop thinking about the past marriage relationship and the circumstances leading to its end. It is natural to give time to reflection after a divorce, and a review of the relationship actually promotes the healing process. Such reflection, however, should not consume every moment of one's day. An intervention developed by de Shazer (1985), called "Write, Read, and Burn," frequently helps depressed individuals who are troubled by obsessive ruminations.

Counselees are instructed to set aside a specific hour, the same time each day, during which they only concentrate on (for example) the failed marriage. On even-numbered days they write down all memories of the relationship, both good and bad. They write for the full hour, even if it means rewriting the same few sentences over and over again. On odd-numbered days they read the previous day's notes and then burn them. If obsessive ruminations crop up at other times, counselees are instructed to delay the thought until the appointed hour. They repeat the even- and odd-day cycle until the obsessive thoughts abate.

Some individuals have trouble believing that writing, and then reading and burning what they wrote, can serve any purpose; therefore the helper needs to present this intervention to the depressed with conviction. The minister's confidence in the intervention will facilitate counselees' willingness to participate. (A few people resist burning what they write; the pastoral caregiver can encourage them instead to keep their writings in a diary.)

"Write, Read, and Burn" works for several reasons: First, it objectifies counselees' concerns, making them more clear-cut and manageable. Second, it converts the "bad" thoughts from a taboo to a part of each day's tasks. Third, people are less likely to dwell on obsessive thoughts throughout the day when a time has been scheduled for them. Counselees eventually allow more important matters to come to the fore, and the depressed, obsessive ruminations decrease or disappear altogether.

"Write, Read, and Burn" is useful for depressive obsessive thoughts of all sorts—not only those concerning divorce. Rarely do depressed individuals need to use this intervention longer than two or three weeks before the thoughts come under control.

Worry Time

Some depressed people find themselves so overwrought with worry that they spend every counseling session as well as many hours every day obsessed with their concerns. *Worry time* can help them. Caregivers may ask counselees, "How long do you think you will need to worry about your problems each day?" Next the minister suggests, "Let us select a time—the same time every day—when you will worry about your problems. Your task during that period of time will be to try very hard to worry about every-thing that you usually worry about throughout the day. The difference is that you will concentrate your worrying into this one period of time." Counselees may choose a half-hour for worrying each day, say from 4:15 to 4:45 P.M. They only worry during that time—nothing else. When worries overcome them and negative thoughts start to dominate their inner world, they delay those thoughts until their worry time.

For counselees the rationale behind worry time is not to avoid think-ing about the things that trouble them, but to decide when the worrying will occur. They concentrate all of their worrying into a brief period and free the rest of the day to carry on with their lives. Depressed individuals sometimes resist this exercise, believing it cannot work; but, in my experi-ence, those who follow worry time rigorously gain control over their obses-sive ruminations, shorten the time they give to worrying, and ultimately find no further use for it.

When counselees say they no longer need a worry time, urge them to be ready to schedule a brief emergency worry time if their worries crop up—preferably later in the same day. Once again, the purpose of worry time is to minimize negative thinking that clouds and distorts one's sense of reality and to release energy for positive endeavors.

Yellow Tablet Analysis

Years ago one of my professors described some Christians as those who "analyze until they paralyze." He was talking about those scrupulous Christians who turn over every action, feeling, and thought, no matter how small, looking for sin. They can ruminate for hours, days, weeks, even years, rehashing their feelings, analyzing themselves and events in their lives. I usually ask such people, "Is this helping you become less depressed?" Nearly all agree it does not. "Then," I suggest, "stop doing it. If it doesn't work, don't do it." Analyzing until you paralyze is not helpful; in fact it is harm-ful. Feelings foster further feelings, and overanalysis of events and the feel-ings that arise from them only lead to deeper depression.

Some depressed individuals will protest that they are searching for truth; they are merely trying to be honest with themselves. I tell them that little truth can be found mucking about in a depressed state. What is more, their ruminations distort thinking and drive them in the opposite direction of honesty and truth. *Depression does not need to be analyzed to be managed!* It is better for counselees to invest their energy in creating work-able solutions.

For those who will not give up analysis, two variations of worry time may help. In one, counselees do their analysis at a specific time each day— but only at that specific time—say 3:00 to 4:00 in the afternoon. In a second variation, whenever counselees slip into analysis, they must do it only with a yellow tablet in their hands, recording their analysis on the tablet. I also change their task from analysis of feelings to analysis of how they can manage their depression. The only back-looking analysis allowed is searching for triggers of their depressed feelings or strengths they are ignoring; the important thing is to move toward the future.

Positive Thinking

Thought stopping. Worry time. Write, read, and burn. Yellow tablet analysis. Even though each of these methods mitigates the damage caused by negative thoughts, they do not necessarily bring about positive ones. It is useful for pastoral caregivers to have a method or two on tap that can promote positive thinking. For counselees who do not recognize their accomplishments, daily reviewing what they have actually achieved—and, for the time being, ignoring what they have not—will help. If they tend to forget their accomplishments, they should record them on a card, carry it around with them, and periodically read the card to help them focus on what they have done.

Depressed people can gain control over thoughts that have become their master through any of these methods to combat obsessive ruminations. Hopefully, too, they can redirect the wasted energy of obsessive thinking toward more productive pursuits.

Transforming How Depressives Think

Certainly one way to strengthen the depressed is to help them think differently. This chapter has discussed cognitive restructuring and obsessive thought procedures; there are other ways to change how people think. Below are listed several additional counseling interventions that change the depressed's negative view of events. No caregiver—clergy or otherwise— would use all of these counseling methods. Instead, choose one or two and try them with depressed counselees. I have used each of these methods at one time or another and have found them useful in pastoral counseling.

Dis-Identification

Many depressed individuals personalize their depression. It is difficult not to do so when you feel terrible. Nevertheless, one of the tasks of the minister is to help *separate the person from the depression.* Melancholics feel miserable; it does not follow that they are miserable creatures. (That would be emotional reasoning.) We all are infinitely worthwhile human beings saved by God's grace, but what we do is not so pure. "For I do not do the good I want, but the evil I do not want is what I do," Paul complains in Rom. 7:19. Depressed individuals tend to mix up being and doing. The task of the minister is to help people dis-identify who they are from what they do. In such a way, they can externalize the experience of depression and separate it from their own infinite worth as children of God. As Michael White points out (1987), the person is not the problem; the *problem* is the problem.

A counseling intervention from the school of psychosynthesis, known as *dis-identification* or *self-identification,* can help depressed individuals to separate who they are from what they do. Roberto Assagioli (1965, 22) maintains that "We are dominated by everything with which our self becomes identified. We can dominate and control everything from which we dis-identify ourselves." I have found his method of dis-identification helpful for people who are very self-critical. The purpose of the method is to help depressed individuals separate themselves from their negative, depressive emotions, thoughts, or desires—recognizing that they have them but are not defined by them. The depressed ultimately see themselves as infinitely precious to God, even though they may have difficulty believing it, and infinitely worthful persons for whom Christ died.

In dis-identification, pastors instruct counselees to relax (using relaxation methods if necessary) and then dis-identify with their body, emotions, and intellect through detailed imaging of an internal dialogue. For example: "I have a body, but I am not my body." "I have an emotional life, but I am not my emotions or feelings." "I have desires, but I am not those desires." "I am lonely much of the time, but that loneliness is not me." In the session—and later on their own—they apply these formulas to anything they have falsely identified as themselves, such as their roles in life, their depressed feelings, their own self-image, their misdeeds, and so forth. Finally, they insert a positive assertion such as: "I am a child of God. I am an infinitely worthful person."

Depressed individuals practice the dis- and self-identification statements for ten or fifteen minutes twice a day, in a relaxed position with their eyes closed, imagining and repeating the mental dialogue. This ritual of dis-identification is helpful only with mildly depressed counselees who are generally healthy but desire greater directedness and control over their lives—especially those who feel they are dominated by particular feelings, thoughts, objects, or individuals.

The Blowup Method

Blowup asks counselees to exaggerate their disturbing negative thoughts to such an extent that they no longer seem awesome and may even appear ludicrous. This counseling intervention is enhanced by closing one's eyes and imaging a troublesome situation in which such negative thoughts may occur. Then the counselees mentally exaggerate the whole situation while describing in the first person what they are thinking, feeling, seeing, and experiencing.

It bears repeating that terminating negative thoughts does not necessarily bring about positive ones—especially among those whose depression is severe. Melancholics need to learn new, positive, reality-based ways of thinking.

The Alternative Technique

Some individuals systematically interpret all events in a negative way. Using the *alternative technique*, pastoral caregivers explain to their depressed counselees the six cognitive information-processing errors that people frequently make (listed at the beginning of this chapter). Together they discuss specific experiences, coming up with new explanations and interpretations of the events (other than those previously formed).

Sulinda, for example, notices that her husband is withdrawn and uncommunicative. She interprets this negatively, convincing herself that he no longer cares for her and may even have a lover. Her pastor urges her to explore alternatives. Perhaps he is suffering a fresh wave of grief over the loss of their child fifteen years ago and does not want to add to Sulinda's troubles by sharing his feelings. He may be up for a promotion at the factory and wonders if he is adequate to the job. Or the impending death of his mother (which Sulinda has mentioned in passing) is weighing on him heavily. Or his company will be downsizing, the IRS is auditing his taxes, he is tired from working two jobs, he has worries about his health. The possibilities are almost infinite. Sulinda must recognize that she needs to obtain accurate information, take charge of her feelings, and reach out to him.

When the depressed recognize their negative biases and substitute more accurate interpretations of their experiences, it becomes a basis for future problem solving. Counselees consider and strategize alternative ways of handling problems based on a new interpretation of the circumstances.

Reattribution

A cognitive method similar to the alternative technique, *reattribution* helps depressed counselees to assign blame or responsibility for negative events more accurately. Working together with the pastoral caregiver, they discuss selected events in their lives. By applying logic, common sense, and a sound understanding of ethics to a variety of negative incidents, counselees try to determine realistic causes. The goal is not to absolve them of responsibility but to note the multitude of extraneous factors that can contribute to any negative event. Reattribution helps people to lift the weight of self-reproach, to search for ways of salvaging troublesome situations, and to prevent recurrences. It can assist parishioners to accept responsibility for real transgressions but not take blame for imagined sins.

Reattribution of major negative events (such as a divorce) can be followed by the historic pastoral methods of confession, forgiveness, absolution, and amendment of life. The pastor should be alert, however, for a dangerous pattern that Roy Fairchild (1980, 33) suggests some Christians learn: "They [the depressed persons] move from guilty feelings to atonement to attempted redemption by placating and obeying, by overworking, by denying themselves pleasure, and by subtle self-sabotage or clear self-destruction." Scrupulosity can replace acceptance of God's forgiveness.

Recent tendencies in the church to minimize or even ignore sin, except as a feature of a global social issue, is an immense loss for depressives. Most feel they are very sinful and have done wrong (and indeed they *are* sinful and have done wrong). The minister who does not believe in personal sin or offers assurance of grace prematurely, glibly, or cheaply, fails to take the depressed or their experience of guilt seriously. To the degree that this occurs, the depressed are left to grapple with their gnawing guilt alone, unaided by their religious adviser. The counseling method of reattribution can serve as a prelude to acceptance of forgiveness for wrongs that really have taken place.

Spiritual Direction

One ancient, historic pastoral care method continues in practice today. *Spiritual direction* is a constructive way to empower those who are depressed. Because they tend to be self-absorbed, melancholics focus their thoughts on themselves and how they relate to other people or events. Spiritual direction allows the depressed to focus on the Ultimate, beyond themselves. It is a way to continue to develop and extend their relationship to God.

A variety of spiritual disciplines have developed in the Christian tradition; some of them I have covered in greater detail elsewhere (Stone 1996). In their caring ministry to the depressed, pastors may wish (once counselees are familiar with spiritual direction and the contemplative attitude) to introduce a variation of the *lectio divina*. (For an introduction to *lectio divina*, I suggest Michael Casey's *Sacred Reading* 1995.) First the depressed need to quiet themselves, perhaps by way of relaxation exercises, imaging, or regularized breathing. For those who already are fairly relaxed, a breathing exercise done with the eyes closed can be a good way to begin. They may count their breaths, or mentally say, "I am," on the inhale and "calm" (or "relaxed") on the exhale. After a few minutes they can move on to the Jesus Prayer ("Jesus Christ, Son of God, have mercy on me, a sinner") or another *monologia*, again in concert with their breathing.

Counselees then slowly read a short passage from the Bible several times over. The psalms are a good place to begin, as well as a system of readings that follow the pattern set forth in Ignatius's description of a religious retreat. When reading the indicated portion of Scripture, counselees reflect on the passage and listen for the Word being spoken to them. The process should not be forced; it is important to stay in the receptive mode, to be patient, not to demand or strive for immediate, earthshaking revelations. This is in the spirit of a verse of an old hymn:

I ask no dream, no prophet ecstasies
No sudden rending of this veil of clay
No angel visitant, no opening skies
But take the dimness of my soul away. (LBW #486)

The final step requires that practitioners close their eyes and again become aware of their breathing. Now, instead of repeating the Jesus Prayer or a monologia, they use phrases from the given Scripture selection to coordinate with their breathing. For example, Psalm 23 (NEB) might be used, beginning as follows:

Inhale: The Lord is my shepherd;
Exhale: I shall want nothing.

Inhale: He makes me lie down in green pastures;
Exhale: I shall want nothing.

Inhale: [He] leads me beside the waters of peace;
Exhale: I shall want nothing.

Inhale: He renews life within me;
Exhale: I shall want nothing.

A prayer forms from those phrases of the Scripture passage that seem especially compelling. Counselees need not worry about forgetting the exact wording or even whole sections of the reading. They will remember the most striking passages in their essence, and these become the prayer. Counselees let these remembered passages, now a prayer, speak to them— in feelings, images, ideas, or memories—and thus listen for the Word, for God present and speaking. The Word continues to speak as they reread and pray the Scripture in the ensuing days and weeks.

The value of such an exercise for depressives is that when they undertake it seriously they do not dwell on their own problems but concentrate on what the Word is saying to them. With those who are cognitively distorting their experiences, I first go over the passage in the session, where we have a chance to talk about it together, and I help them catch distortions in their interpretations. For example, the person who thinks forgiveness is only for other people is urged to apprehend what is freely offered to all, irrespective of how heinous the sin may appear.

One caution in the use of spiritual direction: some depressives may use it as yet another way to pull away from other people, or through it they may become obsessed with their own sin and unworthiness. Be careful that the uses of Scripture, prayer, meditation, contemplation, or the offices do not become another excuse for the depressed to retreat from the world around them. For them, spiritual direction must lead into a positive relationship with God.

Re-Explaining Experience

"Give me an explanation why your friend did not call you last night as he usually does." When you ask depressed individuals such a question, they likely give answers such as "He doesn't love me" or "He was out with someone else." After hearing the negative explanation, helpers might ask: "Please give me some other explanations for this event" (he was sick, he had to work late, he was on the telephone with his mother). This method can help melancholics discover that there are a variety of possible explanations for any event. Often they make the mistake of believing the worst, in the absence of accurate information. *Re-explaining experience,* similar to the alternative technique, causes them to recognize that their immediate hypothesis is only one of a long list of possibilities.

As a homework assignment, counselees can go in search of accurate information. They gather as much data as possible—accurate facts, not hearsay. They must ferret out the real cause or causes of an event—if such causes can be determined—rather than allow their negative thinking to interpret an ambiguous situation.

Depression Flowchart

Depressives, we have noted, almost universally lack confidence in themselves and their abilities. The pastoral caregiver might direct such counselees to create a flowchart of something—anything—that they know how to do well, such as taking a shower (Yapko 1996). They detail each step: take off your clothes, hang them on a hook, close the shower curtain, turn on the hot water, turn on the cold water, check the temperature, get in, press the shower knob, and so forth. The caregiver might ask: "What happens if you skip a step or don't know a step, such as how to flip the control knob from tub to shower? Are you unable to take a shower?"

After counselees write up a flowchart of the linear steps in an everyday task, the helper goes on: "Next I would like you to write up a flowchart of how you get depressed. Think of a recent event that led you into a tailspin. Be very specific and note each step that you took to become depressed. Be sure to include how you handled ambiguous information (for example, your boyfriend didn't call you as he usually does)."

The purpose of writing a depression flowchart is to help people learn about the specific process by which they slip into melancholia and to help them understand the cognitive or behavioral mistakes they make so that they can learn another way of responding to similar events. "Now that you have written a flow chart of how you get depressed, come up with ways in which you can avoid falling into the traps of global thinking, negative attribution, and the like."

Computer illiterates can learn to use a computer if they follow a step-by-step flowchart of the specific keystrokes and mouse clicks needed to turn on a computer and operate a word-processing program. In a similar way people learn how they get depressed in order to design an alternative way of responding to events. By writing a depression flowchart, melancholics can learn a different way of responding to frustrations and ambiguities in life.

Guilt Overload

Yet another counseling method to address information-processing errors, *guilt overload,* directs counselees who feel guilty most of the time to choose several recent events from the paper, such as a train crash in Turkey. Next the pastoral caregiver instructs them "write a paragraph on how you caused it" (Yapko 1996). They must describe in considerable detail how they caused the Turkish train to crash. Obviously this is ridiculous. The purpose for such a task is to help counselees see how ridiculous it is for them to feel guilty for things over which they have little or no control.

For counselees who invest tremendous energy trying to control what is not controllable, and thus feel guilty for failing to do so, I may say: "In the coming week, I would like you to help your son [whose musical appreciation is limited to rap music] to develop a taste for jazz. I want you to try every way possible to get him to like it." This is an impossible task. They will fail. Such an exercise would have been useful for the mother (discussed earlier) who was upset because her daughter was not accepted in the college of her choice. It leads to a discussion of what we can and cannot control. Guilt overload tasks may not change the situation, but they can change how counselees think about it.

The Inner Critic

Everyone seems to have an *inner critic*. It is the voice inside your head that tells you terrible things about yourself, things you never admit to anyone else. One of the things I have observed in years of counseling depressed individuals is that they are very attentive to this inner critic. Some almost seem to worship their inner critic, paying more attention to it than to God or anyone else. I have often thought that I should create an idol of that inner critic—possibly one for each gender—since so many people worship their inner critic as much or more than any god, and the attention that depressives pay to their inner critic is tantamount to idolatry.

Those who are not particularly depressed, who tend to feel good about themselves, may listen momentarily to their inner critic, assess whether it has any validity in reality, ignore it or take care of it, and move on with life. Depressed individuals listen and believe whatever their inner critic has to say. An exercise to help address this idolatry of the inner critic is as follows (Yapko 1996):

1. "Close your eyes and allow your inner critic to talk to you for a minute or so. Listen to what it is saying and be aware of what you feel."

2. "Now think of a funny voice (Daffy Duck, Ross Perot, Mickey Mouse). Give this inner critic that voice and let it continue talking to you." The result is an auditory shift. The inner critic is not saying anything different; only its voice has changed.

3. "Now, with your eyes still closed, have the voice come from a different place, like your armpit or your belly button or your big toe. What happens when your inner critic speaks to you through your belly button?"

This is a spatial shift. The critical voice of the inner critic is still there, but in the matter of a few minutes the frame has changed. As a result, the counselee is listening to the critic differently.

Counselees usually laugh and think the exercise is funny. I urge them to consider that if in the matter of just a few minutes they can change this one aspect of their depression, then they can change others as well. Remember, the goal of pastoral counseling is not necessarily to eradicate depression, but to *manage* it. By giving the inner, critical negative ruminations the voice of Mickey Mouse, who speaks out of an armpit, depressed individuals can learn to exercise some control over what they thought was uncontrollable.

Options

Melancholics believe they have little or no agency, that there is nothing they can do. Many also tend to be rigid in their thinking, viewing every event or situation as either/or, black and white. Therefore it is helpful to urge them—almost force them—to list a variety of optional viewpoints, perspectives, or ways of doing things. For example, consider the depressed husband who is trapped in his low-paying job and unable to advance to the position he would like because he did not finish college; yet he believes his wife should not work outside the home. His homework is to write a variety of ways in which some other man in his situation might handle it. He is to look at other people at work, in his church, among his friends, to see (or hypothesize) how they would unravel the fix he is in. He must write down at least five different ways in which his dilemma could be resolved.

The options exercise can apply to a variety of situations or events. Counselees do not have to agree with the options they have discovered, just write them down. The purpose of the exercise is to expand people's flexibility and help them at least to consider alternative courses of action, thus loosening their rigidity and allowing them to experience their agency. Hope is generated as they consider other futures.

Resignation

One of the tasks of bereaved persons in the weeks and months after the loss of a significant relationship is learning to let go, to release their attachments to the dead. It is a recognition that one can no longer have what once was precious, yet that their lives can have meaning in spite of that great loss. *Resignation* is a natural part of the grief process.

Learning how people resign themselves to a loved one's death is beneficial for melancholics, especially for those who worry excessively about the future or whose expectations are out of proportion to their skills and abilities. Their helpless feelings may actually be realistic; perhaps they do not have the abilities, skills, or wherewithal to obtain the outcomes they desire. Resignation involves finding more realistic expectations for themselves, of the world and others; changing some of their unrealistic assumptions or expectations; choosing alternative goals to work for; and discovering new sources for meaning in life. It does *not* involve resigning themselves to helplessness. They also need to acquire whatever new skills they need to cope with the loss of old dreams and goals. I, for example, have always been an athlete. Tennis was my game. But, with two "blown" knees, I had to resign myself to give up the game entirely and replace it with boring workouts in the gym. Chess anyone?

Reframing Perfectionism

Perfectionists who are depressed drag out all of their old mistakes and dwell upon them. They dig up the past and look at awful decisions they made in marriage, poor choices of schools or majors, bad investment decisions, or even such small events as not getting to a concert on time. Dwelling on these mistakes pulls them into depression's undertow.

Bandler and Grinder (1979) suggest that helpers adjust the distorted thinking of such perfectionistic melancholics by reframing a "mistake" as "the best choice at the time." The aim is to help counselees recognize that at the particular time when they decided on a spouse, a job, an apartment, or what time to leave for the concert, they made the best decision they could, given the available information. To criticize themselves from hindsight serves no benefit and in fact is unrealistic. Such counselees need to accept that most decisions, however wrong they turned out, were the best they could do with what they knew (or thought they knew, in their depressed condition) at the time. No one can divine the future; we make the choices we can, learn from bad decisions, and move into the future.

Clearly this particular reframe is not appropriate for people who have made bad and often irresponsible decisions based not upon lack of information, but upon willfulness, greed, anger, alcohol and other drugs, or lust. This is not "the best they could do at the time." Deliberate and willful acts need to be addressed as such.

Be Kind to a Depressed Person

When you ask husbands or wives if they can tell you their spouses' faults, virtually all of them can provide lists of some length—yet they still love their mates. In fact, their marriages may flourish. The depressed, however, do not know how to face their own faults and also love themselves. One way to care for depressed individuals is to help them learn to treat themselves as kindly as they would treat those whom they love in spite of their foibles.

The point has been made throughout this book that the depressed treat themselves badly, sometimes harshly. They are highly self-critical, ruminate over their mistakes, and cognitively distort most of their experience negatively. To some depressed individuals I will say something like, "I'm thankful you don't treat others as you treat yourself. If you did, you would be very cruel. You would not give them the compassion, tenderness, and respect they deserve. (Pause.) I would like to see you treat yourself with the same dignity, respect, and compassion that you treat others."

Sometimes it takes considerable effort to convince depressed persons that they are worthy of tenderness or compassion. They may subscribe to the growth-from-suffering school and tell you that from their journey of pain they are growing as persons. It is important to help them distinguish between pain that they have not caused, which can bring about personal growth (Frankl 1963), and the useless self-pummeling that brings about no growth, no change, no insight, but rather a life of personal abuse and anguish.

We have examined the many ways in which melancholics distort their perceptions. Whether the depression is physiological or psychological in origin, faulty thinking can perpetuate despair. Change is possible through an array of pastoral counseling methods that restructure cognitions, stop obsessive ruminations, and bring the dynamics of depression under control.

The goal is not necessarily to eradicate depression (a daunting or perhaps even impossible task) but to manage it, confine it, and limit its impact on people's lives. The depressed can learn to treat themselves with consideration and kindness. Even relapses lose their terror once depressives realize how to control them. When negative ruminations are replaced with positive thinking, renewed life lies before them—life filled with dangers, to be sure, but also with meaning and purpose. Acting as agents of renewed life through their pastoral care and counseling ministry, pastors thereby fulfill the very essence of their calling.

TEN | **Behavioral Interventions: Shifting from Passive to Active Mode**

For good reason, "the doldrums" is a familiar metaphor for depression. Even occasional sailors are familiar with the phenomenon; the water is like glass, there is no wind at all. Without a motor, the boat sits motionless in the water, the boom swings dangerously back and forth, the sails flutter but fail to catch any wind. Likewise melancholics often are motionless, powerless, dead in the water. They have a tendency to avoid or escape the usual routines of life. There is no wind in their sails.

As a result, people who are depressed cope poorly with practical everyday problems. The simplest tasks are exhausting. They may act like they are giving up on everything. (Although the vast majority of melancholics reduce normal activity, a few become agitated or hyperactive and may engage in aggressive or compulsive acts.)

Melancholia is a vicious circle (*spiral* might be a better word). A reduction in activities with positive outcomes can lead to depressed feelings; these feelings lead to decreased interest in activities that might have positive outcomes, which leads to fewer positive outcomes and thus to even greater depression, and so on. Reversing this downward spiral calls for the intervention of caregivers who guide the depressed into positive movement. Improved performance in activities leads to improved self-evaluation and increases the motivation to do even more, which leads to improved performance, and so on. Therefore one way for pastoral caregivers to help melancholics is to blow a little breeze into their sails—to get them active whether they feel like it or not. They act their way into a new way of feeling.

Getting Active

Many melancholics feel as if they are floating and powerless—and then do what they feel like doing, which is nothing. Or they wait for the perfect goal or the right direction; uncertain of what that is, they go nowhere at all. Like sailors in the doldrums, the depressed need to find a bit of breeze and get moving; they need to exercise some control over their environment. Their destination may be important ultimately, but at this stage direction is less important than movement.

Passivity and inaction are major obstacles for those who suffer depression. It is not always an easy task to get them to act, but when they do, they begin to feel at least slightly better. They may ignore these improved feelings or even see them as unimportant exceptions to their depression, so an ancillary task of the pastoral caregiver is to point out how their mood has lifted. Often the depressed make the mistake of waiting until they have enough motivation to act. This is a big mistake. Like some would-be artists and writers waiting for inspiration before taking brush to canvas or pen to paper, many who are depressed assume that they need to feel like doing something before they can do it. Therefore they produce little or nothing, for ennui is integral to depression.

Studies of successful people show that they work whether they feel inspired or not. In fact, many productive people rarely experience inspiration before they do a task. Frequently their motivation arises out of doing the task itself. (In more than thirty years of writing I have produced only four pages of manuscript that came from pure inspiration. An editor cut out two of them.) Remember the law of inertia: not only does a body at rest tend to remain at rest; *a body in motion tends to remain in motion.* Therefore pastoral caregivers need to encourage their depressed parishioners not to act according to their depressed feelings, which will only lead to inactivity, but to do what they know they should do whether they feel like it or not. This is ethical behavior. It is convenient to feel like doing the right thing, but even if you don't, the ethical response is (in the words of humorist Garrison Keillor) to "get up and do what needs to be done."

Two counseling processes can stir depressed individuals out of their passivity. One helps them structure activities at which they can be effective. A second prompts them to look at what they have already done or are presently doing, and recognize their own competence. (The latter calls for cognitive methods, discussed in chapter 9.)

Some depressed individuals see all of life as an either/or, all-or-nothing situation; their expectations are so elevated that they could not achieve them even if they were feeling happy and confident. The minister can use cognitive methods to help such people trim their expectations so they can move effectively (and realistically) into action.

Homework Tasks

Assisting the depressed to become more active usually requires homework tasks. Ideally, homework tasks are negotiated between pastor and counselee, but they may be assigned. (In cases where the depression is quite deep, it may be necessary to prescribe the first assignments, later guiding the counselees to a more active part in determining the tasks.) Encourage counselees to write down precisely what homework they have agreed to do and at what time. I ask those who are very withdrawn or are significantly distorting reality to read back the assignments, making sure the homework task is clear to both of us.

Next the depressed must actually do their tasks, thus taking small steps that lead to success. If the depression is advanced, some of the early homework assignments need to be very small and easily achievable. These people do not need another failure!

Some of these first assignments may seem inconsequential, but to the depressed they are rigorous. The minister must be sure counselees are not attempting too big a leap, one at which they are likely to fail. For example, a woman who needed to get out of the house every morning first agreed to weed the garden, and later the yard. Her hour of weeding was a big step from lying in bed or sitting inside the house all day. Later, she was able to go on to more difficult tasks.

Control

People need control in order to change and take action. Change occurs because people exercise mastery over their environment. Successful people are not afraid to use their power. To become successful in overcoming depression, counselees need to distinguish between what they can (and should) control and what they cannot (or should not) control—and to invest their energies appropriately.

Sometimes control is crucial. Writing a book is a control-favorable situation. I have to seize ideas and fashion them into a semblance of order and coherence for the book to have value—let alone get published. When I am trying to get my wife to do what I want her to do, it is a control-unfavorable situation. Although I can negotiate vigorously for the change

I want—and I do that—I also need to respect what she wants. I cannot control her if she does not want it.

As a rule, melancholics either overcontrol or undercontrol their situations (Yapko 1994). In my experience, undercontrol is the more common problem. Those who do not exert control where they could or should do so operate from a victim's mindset. Yapko (ibid., 107) describes the victim mentality as "global, other-directed, open, enmeshed, people oriented, extrapunitive, ambiguous about personal values and personal worth, highly reactive, past oriented, and low in ability to compartmentalize." Martin Seligman (1973, 1974, 1983) performed several studies on *learned helplessness*. Subjects were given an uncontrollable negative stimulus; no matter what they tried to do, they could not escape it. Later the environment was restructured so that they could escape the negative stimulus, but the participants no longer tried to escape. They had learned helplessness. Seligman argues that depressives act like the subjects of the experiment—they stop trying to control things in a favorable way. They feel, and therefore become, helpless and hopeless.

Not all melancholics are undercontrolling victims. Overcontrollers attempt to master situations that are not controllable. They try to bring about change when change is not within their power. They fail, of course, and slide into depression. In fact, some very competent people, highly successful in their work, experience depression related to overcontrol. For example, a corporate executive may handle everything at her job with consummate skill and authority, but when she returns home each day to her spouse and applies the same methods of control, it is a dismal failure. Yapko (1994) lists characteristics of people who overcontrol as "excessive guilt, intrapunitive, concrete, internal locus of control, enmeshed, linear, and task oriented." High achievers frequently determine their worth by what they do; they expect nothing short of excellence in every area of their lives. No matter how successful they are in one realm, if they fail in another they can become miserably unhappy, depressed individuals.

It is hazardous for the depression-prone to become involved in activities or events over which they have little control. It is better that they invest their energy in things over which they can have some degree of control. A father is in for trouble if he upsets himself because his son has become a professional snowboarder instead of going to college and studying law in order to join the family firm. In our culture and time we cannot control our children's life choices, and such a situation is tailor-made for depression.

Sometimes scaling questions help melancholics discover what they can and cannot control. Ask, for example, "On a scale of one to ten, if zero means you have no control and ten means you have complete control, how much control do you think you have in this situation?" Scaling questions help counselees to determine as accurately as possible the extent of their power, so they can invest their energies successfully and resign themselves to what they cannot manage.

To sum up: two extremes are hazardous for those who are prone to depression. People who believe they have no control in most situations of life are the *victims;* they are primed for depression. Individuals who believe they have (or should have) complete control are also in for trouble. An essential task for caregivers is to help counselees to recognize their finite freedom and to exercise their agency within it.

Obstacles to Getting Active

Unfortunately, many depressed persons simply do not exercise control or take on activities that would help them manage their depression. Besides overcontrolling or undercontrolling, some depressed individuals approach behavioral tasks in other ways that prevent their accomplishment.

The feeling of pressure from tasks undone, ironically, frustrates performance accomplishment. This pleasure-destroying anxiety is common among depressed students, who have difficulty enjoying a movie or reading a novel because they cannot help thinking about all the homework that has yet to be done in the semester. During the last few days of the term this is appropriate and they should be studying; but four, six, or eight weeks into the semester it is not reasonable to expect that all of the term's requirements should be completed before relaxing. The pressure of tasks not completed can sap the little energy depressed individuals have for getting things done.

The same pressure from tasks undone afflicts melancholics who procrastinate. Lacking energy and gumption, they put off the simplest of chores. As time goes by these chores magnify until they seem large (or even impossible). For example, six weeks before he is to move, a depressed man may note that he should send his address change to the post office. Feeling too tired to call for the proper form, he tells himself he will do it tomorrow. Three weeks after the move, tomorrow still waits. His affairs are a mess because of lost and misdirected mail, and the undone task looms malevolently over every chance for enjoyment.

Frequently the depressed do not take care in choosing tasks, falling into activities which do not interest them rather than undertaking what might give them enjoyment, meaning, or a sense of adequacy. Pastoral caregivers should examine carefully with counselees whether the activities they are proposing are really something they would want to do if they were not depressed.

Sometimes the precipitators of a depression (significant crisis, loss, etc.) remove the availability or possibility of quality activities. This is especially true of pleasurable relationships with friends. For example, in grief research done a number of years ago, I found that widowed middle-aged spouses immediately lost half of their friendships when their mates died. Those absent friends (frequently other couples) could have provided sustenance and community through the person's darkest hours of grief. If the bereaved is also depressed, the problem is exacerbated. Since the depressed usually are not as skillful in relationships, friends and even family may drift away—taking with them the possibility of beneficial interpersonal activities.

Anxiety or stress also can affect both the performance of activities and the enjoyment of pleasurable events. Persons who suffer anxiety attacks or significant stress are less likely to experience enjoyment in what they do, especially if they are depressed (Lewinsohn 1978). Sometimes ministers need to address both moods—anxiety and depression—in their counseling.

The following principles should be kept in mind when assigning homework designed to overcome some of the typical obstacles to becoming active:

• Help the depressed recognize that *doing* something, not achieving something, is most critical.

• Sometimes, what a person is able to accomplish is determined by *external factors* as much as, if not more than, by internal ones. (For example, while learning to be assertive is generally helpful, one's employer may be afraid of such behavior and make things more difficult because of the employee's assertiveness.)

• The *either/or thinking* of many depressives leads them to believe they must do every iota of what they have planned. If they cannot, they feel even worse and assume their time and effort were wasted. The minister must help them trim expectations and view their progress realistically. Cognitive restructuring may be called for (chapter 9).

• Sometimes it is helpful, especially for the more severely depressed, to *schedule daily activities* on an hour-by-hour basis, or even in fifteen-minute blocks if that seems appropriate. The section Structuring Daily Tasks (page 137) will give more details. For those who are quite depressed, accomplishing a few basic maintenance activities around the house is all that should be expected.

Helpful Activities for the Depressed

Certain types of activities are especially helpful for depressives. People who perform these or similar actions tend to feel better and have less depression than those who do not. They include:

• *Interpersonal activities* (see chapter 7) in which the depressed feel appreciated, accepted, valued, and liked. For example, a depressed amateur radio operator shows his radio gear to some interested novices, a lonely single person makes a point of being among people who are enjoying a mutual good time, an elderly widower finds others who show interest in his hobbies.

• Activities in which the depressed can demonstrate *competence, independence, and adequacy* (for example, undertaking a special project at work that is beyond the normal requirements of the job and allows creativity and independence).

• *Enjoyable* activities that contain intrinsic pleasure (or would, when the melancholic person is not depressed) such as going out for dinner at a fine restaurant, lying on the beach, going to a favorite sporting event, or taking a drive in the country to see the autumn colors.

• Activities that help counselees gain a *sense of meaning in life.* Melancholics frequently have difficulty sensing any purpose for their existence. Victor Frankl (1963) observed that those who are able to see meaning in their lives—even in a concentration camp, as he was—have less tendency to depression and more energy for carrying on the tasks of existence. He pointed out that meaning does not come to us out of the blue, but we must seek it, strive for it, carve it out. Meaning is crucial for survival. In the concentration camp, Frankl noted, those who did not find meaning in their existence inevitably died.

People who see their lives as connected to something greater than themselves are less likely to suffer depression. This something can be a social cause, a happy marriage, volunteering to tutor disadvantaged children, or a deep commitment to one's faith group and relationship to God. Counselees who find meaning in their lives, and put meaning into action, are better able to manage their depression.

Interpersonal, competence enhancing, enjoyable, and meaning-filled activities help depressed individuals become active participants in life. They are not fillers for their idle time but help them get out of the doldrums, catch the wind, and sail in a more purposeful direction.

Counseling Methods to Change Behavior

Clearly certain specific behaviors exacerbate depression. Likewise other behaviors, if practiced, help ameliorate the distress. Therefore it is valuable to help the depressed to make behavioral changes that will improve their frame of mind and better manage their depression. The following counseling methods help the depressed move into a more active mode of existence.

Confidence Building

A program of confidence building (what Yapko calls the "Becoming More Confident Program") helps elevate depressives' estimation of themselves and their abilities (Yapko 1994). Counselees are instructed first to explore past activities that have helped them become more confident, and therefore less depressed, and brainstorm other ways of building their confidence. Reviewing what has worked in the past may take up a significant portion of one counseling session. Ask many questions. Let counselees educate you: "Let's explore what specific things you have done whenever your depression got better. It can help us understand what you can do to manage your depression now." Focus on their strengths and past successes.

Be careful: many counselees will say "nothing worked" or "I just came out of it; I didn't do anything to make it better." Or they will return to negative events in the past rather than looking at what they have done that has helped them manage the depression.

Pastoral caregivers and counselees together structure a confidence-building program, listing specific steps they will take. Write down the tasks, then let counselees choose the first steps they will take as homework to be completed before their next counseling session. Subsequent sessions begin by reviewing the program and evaluating what specific actions seem to be providing the greatest benefits.

Quick-Action Plan

Often it is useful to develop a quick-action plan for the period after the depression lifts. Remember that depression comes back about 50% of the time. After suffering through one episode, most individuals prefer to ignore signs of its return. Nevertheless, it is unwise to dismiss signs of recurrent depression, for if they are recognized early, the sufferer has more psychic energy available to follow a plan of prevention.

Here is a plan that works for many. On a small card, counselees write a statement such as the following: "If I begin to feel sad (depressed) in the future, I agree to do at least two of the following immediately." (This sentence may include specific signs of recurring depression such as not returning phone calls or skipping meals.) Below it, they list behaviors that have helped them with present or past periods of depression, as well as other actions that they predict will be useful in managing it. I may add suggestions of actions that have helped others. The following are sample items for the card:

1. Go tell someone (spouse or friend) about it.
2. Continue or increase cardiovascular exercises.
3. See my minister (physician, psychiatrist, pastoral counselor) immediately.
4. Go out to lunch with a friend.
5. Renew taking my antidepressant pills.
6. Go to Saturday breakfast meetings of the men's group at church.

Counselees carry the card with them at all times. If they begin to feel depressed, they choose at least two items from the list and begin to do them *the same day.*

Those suffering from melancholia have trouble choosing a beneficial course and then following it. The quick-action plan lists decisions they have made beforehand, while they were feeling more hopeful and less likely to distort their thinking. It spells out actions to be taken on the first day that signs of depression appear.

Take on a Family Member's Depression

Family members can provide valuable support for behavioral change. Cloe Madanes (1984, 173) tells of counseling a young woman who, it seemed, could not break out of her depression. Madanes directed the woman's father to take over her depression for a few days so that she could be free to pursue other interests and get some things done.

Family members so instructed must act weighted down, sad, and helpless. The depressed are then told that they have a week's reprieve and should accomplish as much as they can during the break.

Often melancholics who have handed over their suffering for a time discover they have more agency than they realized—that their depression is subject to change and management. They are able to accomplish more, and the increased accomplishments can lead them to feeling better. It also provides family members with some insight into the experience of depression. Ultimately the depressed person and the family members discover that the depression is more controllable than previously thought.

Work outside the Home

Another method that deals with behaviors, especially for depressed persons who are unemployed, retired, or at home with their children, is to *find* paid or volunteer *employment*. Work outside the home confers a number of benefits. It gets folks out of bed in the morning. It causes them take care of their appearance. It lets them help other people. It provides a structure for their days. It usually places them in an environment where they must interact with other people. It requires that they carry out certain activities whether they feel like it or not. Any work outside of the home, therefore, has considerable potential to get the depressed out of the doldrums.

Structuring Daily Tasks

Individuals who choose to stay at home need at least to structure their days. In extreme cases their assignments can be as basic as getting out of bed, showering, and dressing. Sometimes it helps to have counselees sit down at night or the first thing in the morning and write a list of tasks that they commit to doing during the day ahead. The list includes only what they can reasonably expect to accomplish in one day: the tasks *must* be doable, basic, and very specific. Those who do not want to take on much at first might begin nominally, each day adding one very small task that will stretch them a little and offer a greater sense of accomplishment. Be sure to urge counselees not to judge the value of the tasks they are doing, but simply do them.

Diversion

Diversion serves those who find that their depression is most pronounced during a certain part of the day (typically the morning) or week (typically weekends). The pastoral caregiver helps them plan diversionary tactics for such times. For example, every morning Earl, a retired man who lived alone, felt very depressed and had difficulty facing his work around the house. The method he developed to deal with his depression was to get up early, finish all his chores by 8 A.M., and leave the house until noon. Getting out of the house did not always mean going to some other location; it could be nothing more than tending his garden or sitting in a lawn chair and reading. Earl's morning diversionary tactics were, in my assessment, one of the major aids in managing his depression—especially at first, until he experienced some success and felt better.

Teach Me How to Get Depressed

Melancholics experience a lack of agency. That is, they feel powerless to change what is happening to them. Nothing works. They have no options. They are trapped in their depression. One way to help such counselees gain a degree of control over their depression is to put them in the role of teacher. I once counseled a successful, thirty-three-year-old bank examiner who seemed to have everything going for him—including a supportive wife and a charming seven-year-old son—yet he was depressed. This man had experienced several previous periods of depression that lasted from two to six months. After our opening conversation, I said to him: "It seems to me that you have learned much about depression through your own experiences of it. I would like you to teach me how to get depressed. Help me understand how you do it."

He replied with a rehash of everything he had already told me; he thought that depression just came over him and left him unable to change anything in his work, his home, or his own feelings. This is a typical initial response to the "teach me how to get depressed" challenge. Try asking more specific questions, such as: What is your particular method of getting depressed? What things do you do just before you start feeling depressed? What do you do the first thing in the morning? Right after work? Late at night? What do you stop doing? What words do you say to yourself? How do you work/eat/dress/talk/play differently?

Once counselees articulate the concrete mechanics of becoming depressed, the next step is to direct questions toward those times when their depression recedes: What things do you do just before these bad feelings start easing off? What actions seem to reduce the impact of your depressive feelings upon your work or your home life? How do you finally get to the point where you are tired of sitting around and decide to go back to playing golf with your buddies?

The purpose of such questioning, besides making counselees aware of specific behaviors that lead them into depression, is to help them recognize that they have some control over their melancholia—or at least over how they respond to it. By the conscious choice of certain activities, depressed individuals can lessen the impact of their unhappy condition.

The bank examiner—as one might expect from an accountant—put together a specific and organized list of things he does before becoming depressed (such as working late but getting less done, watching more television, and avoiding sex), as well as concrete actions that precede a lifting of his mood (such as timing tasks to finish them quickly, helping his son

with school work, expressing more affection to his wife). He began following conscientiously his detailed plan of how he gets out of depression and
has learned to stave off melancholy in its initial stages, before feeling its
painful effects and spreading the gloom to those he loves.

Journal Writing

Writing in a personal journal furnishes a potent tool for depressed individuals as they struggle out of their low times. Preserved in the journal,
their *positive* moments (however small) become evidence to be read and
reflected upon during the darkest days, when the misery is too deep to
allow the recognition of the many events in their lives that give them
meaning, pleasure, confidence, or control. Daily writing also adds discipline to their life, and the resulting record of activities can help the pastoral caregiver to fine-tune the counselees' homework tasks and to plan
new activities.

Prescribing Depression

Prescribing the actual symptom, or some element of it, is a counseling
method that addresses specific behaviors of those who are depressed (Stone
1994). Symptom prescription can take several forms. In some cases counselees practice the problem symptoms exactly as they exist. Other times the
minister can ask the counselee to exaggerate certain traits of depression or
make minor changes in how they are practiced. In all cases, pastoral caregivers facilitate control over depressive symptoms that were perceived to be
beyond the counselees' control.

Practicing the problem behavior is a first step toward changing it.
Furthermore, many people do not like to be told what to do—not even
things they are already doing! To quote Milton H. Erickson, "The idea is to
make a laborious task out of whatever the habit [symptom] is—you turn a
vicious habit into an awful inconvenience which the [counselee] is willing
to give up" (Rossi et al. 1983, 264).

Erickson (Haley 1973, 197) once treated an adolescent girl who still
sucked her thumb. He did not prescribe the usual deterrents, for they had
already failed. Instead, he instructed the girl to suck her thumb for twenty
minutes each evening in front of her father and after that for twenty minutes in front of her mother. She was to do it in as aggressive and noisy manner as possible. He directed the parents to ignore her completely. Rather
than trying to induce the child to stop sucking her thumb, as so many had
done before him, Erickson modified the way she went about it. She was

supposed to suck her thumb, but only in the way instructed. When a symptom is changed into a duty, most children tire of it quickly. No longer forbidden pleasure or a weapon to use against parents, it loses its appeal, as thumb sucking did for Erickson's young counselee.

If melancholics can be inspired to change certain aspects of their depression in any respect at the bidding of the helper, they are more likely to ascribe to the caregiver the power to change it in other ways as well. By following instructions to modify a symptom, they establish a pattern of assenting to the caregiver's suggestions. This compliance, or "yes-set," sets the stage for subsequent tasks designed to bring about the desired change.

One way to prescribe depression directs counselees to set up a specific time each day as their depression time (Haley, 1973; Stone 1994). The pastoral caregiver may say: "Your job this next week is to feel down in the dumps, like there is no light at the end of the tunnel. You are to wallow in your depression. Feel its many facets. Experience its full impact on your life." Counselees schedule their depression time at the same period each day for a maximum of one hour; afternoon or early evening are especially good. During the scheduled time they do no other tasks nor do they talk with anyone—their only purpose is to feel woefully sad. If they begin to feel unhappiness coming on at other times during the day, they must tell themselves: "Not now—I'll get back to it at four o'clock." From four to five o'clock each day they are inactive, passive, and miserable, but during the rest of the day they must act and focus on concerns other than their depressed feelings.

If counselees find that they have difficulty limiting their depression to a certain time each day, urge them to redouble their efforts, to work even harder at being depressed at the depression time. "Get your spouse and friends to suggest things you should feel depressed about and how you can do a better job of being depressed." The advantage of prescribing depression is that counselees gain a sense of control over their depressed feelings.

Jay Haley (1984) sometimes suggests that caregivers turn a behavior into such an *ordeal* that the counselee does not want to do it anymore. An additional chore or two may be added to the prescription of depression, to make the task even more onerous. For example, counselees may be asked to do a job they have been avoiding, such as cleaning the garage, in their depression time. Or they may use the time to get on the hated exercise bike or stair stepper. While doing the additional task, they think only their depressed thoughts. They actively try to be sad.

There is a variation of symptom prescription that deals directly with a depressed person's thinking. Since the depressed negatively distort cognitions, a symptom prescription that Yapko (1994) calls *pathological interpretations* may be useful. Counselees consider neutral events, such as their choice of clothes for a particular day or what they will eat from a restaurant menu, and then come up with three pathological interpretations of that event. They already are distorting negatively most of the things they do; here the pastoral caregiver asks them to do intentionally what they are already doing unintentionally. It is good to have them write down these pathological interpretations. (Suggest writing them down only to counselees who are certain to do it, however.) After several days, have them reverse the task and come up with positive interpretations for each of these neutral events. As they alternate between pathological and positive interpretations, gradually they recognize that there are a variety of possible interpretations to every event.

Symptom prescription is not applicable to every pastoral counseling situation. It works best with people who can laugh at themselves, and the minister must believe in its efficacy. This is no time for tentativeness; suggesting any form of symptom prescription takes a certain amount of chutzpah if the counselee is to believe it will work.

Helping the Depressed to Do What Needs to Be Done

Changed behavior is a goal of pastoral counseling. When change does not take place, some helpers rationalize that the counselee was insufficiently motivated, resistant, and unwilling to risk the steps necessary for the change to occur. This is true, no doubt, but there is more to the story. Often people do not achieve the desired change because it seems so far beyond their reach that fear or anxiety takes over. They also do not know *how* to do what needs to be done; they lack the needed skills or practice.

People seeking change need a transition between knowing and doing. *Accomplishment rehearsal* enables counselees to do what they need to do but feel powerless to perform. Having them image in their minds how they will accomplish specific tasks sometimes provides the little extra confidence needed to actually do those tasks.

One experiment in accomplishment rehearsal demonstrated the power of imagery. Allen Richardson (Cleve 1989, 171) divided a number of high school basketball players into three groups. The first group was to practice free-throw shots for an hour a day for twenty days. The second group was to do nothing, and the third group was to vividly image themselves practicing free-throw shots for an hour a day for the same twenty days, "watching" the ball all the way into the basket. The result after the twenty-day trial was that the group that practiced for an hour a day improved its free throw shooting by 24%; the group that did not practice at all showed no improvement; and the group that used mental imagery for an hour a day improved by 23%. Accomplishment rehearsal helps individuals change how they do things by visualizing before actually doing.

Behavioral rehearsal (role playing) works much like accomplishment rehearsal, but instead of visualizing a task, counselees practice it in the counseling session. Once counselees are convinced of the value of the desired behavior, explain the method of behavioral rehearsal. Describe it as a dry run, much like practicing a speech in front of a mirror or trying a golf swing without a ball.

Next, encourage them to role-play or rehearse. Do not allow scenes to go on for more than a few minutes; it is better to practice a short scene several times than to do one long one. Usually the new behavior is easily defined and requires little preparation before practicing it. A father can redo a parent-child fight in which he expelled his daughter from the house. In practice, he would start over again and try a different way of handling the disagreement, perhaps several different ways, leading to quite different results. Use as many details as necessary to make the scenes vivid. Instruct those who are redoing a troublesome past event to use the same situational background in a fresh way, not merely replaying the scene but approaching it as if it never happened before.

Sometimes the depressed fail to change simply because they do not know where to begin. At such times, *modeling* or demonstrating the desired behavioral is helpful. Caregivers should offer specifics on how to act differently. For example, I may model for a wife several ways of raising a difficult issue with her husband.

After practicing a scene, two steps remain. First, talk about how well it was played and offer ideas for improvement. Second, clarify how the lessons will be transferred into daily life. Because behavioral rehearsal seeks to help counselees put what they have learned into practice, ask them to spell out exactly what parts of the rehearsed behavior they will actually do in the coming week.

Behavioral rehearsal is a profitable intervention for pastoral counseling of the depressed because those who have first practiced in the counseling session are far more likely to put their new behaviors into practice in real life.

The wrong behaviors—or lack of action—can draw people deeper and deeper into their melancholia. By replacing even some of those neutral or malignant behaviors with positive actions, those who suffer from depression can regain a degree of control over their lives and incrementally improve their state. No longer dead in the water, they find a way out of the doldrums to a little breeze in their sails, to power, movement, hope.

Epilogue

Sometimes depression seems like a demon that fights off interveners. In the real world of spilled milk, blemishes, flat tires, and crying children, people do not always manage their depression or seek solutions to their problems. They may not gain hope for a better future—however skillfully they have been counseled. Sometimes it seems as if they *want* to be depressed, to stay in the past, and to wallow in the mire of their despair.

Why does pastoral counseling sometimes fail? Perhaps the depressed truly do not want to change. Perhaps the minister is of the "wrong" gender, race, nationality, dress size, social status, politics, voice, or accent—for people's prejudices are likely to affect their relationship with any counselor, even their own pastor. Clergy may be less than effective if the counselee is unnervingly like a dysfunctional parent of their own, or if the marital conflicts which have resulted from the depression have a too-familiar ring. Some counselees would do better in a group situation, either within the church or outside of it. They may require a different form of help (such as medical consultation, legal advice, or psychological testing). Whatever the reason, sometimes the help we offer as pastoral caregivers does not benefit those who need it.

Referral

Are parish pastors on the bottom rung of the helping professions, offering cheap but second-rate care to those who suffer from melancholia? Some mental-health professionals and pastoral counseling specialists seem to think so, and a few even hold the view that the only thing ministers should do in cases of depression is to recommend referral.

On the contrary: I am more convinced than ever before that ministers in the parish are offering competent, first-rate care and counsel for those who suffer from depression—far beyond merely recognizing warning signs and dispatching counselees to a specialist. The genius of pastoral caregiving for the depressed lies in the fact that, at its best, it is a team effort. In fact no one is in a better position to give the best possible care and counsel to the depressed, and their families or social systems, because of parish pastors' ongoing relationships, congregational resources, and sensitivity to spiritual struggles; and because as ministers of the Gospel they are messengers of grace, redemption, and hope.

Good pastoral caregiving frequently includes a number of helpers. The team may include primary-care physicians, psychologists, psychiatrists, financial and legal professionals, assistant pastors, lay pastoral caregivers and other church members, the family of the depressed, teachers, school counselors, social workers, probation officers, employers, or even the police. Pastors are in a unique position to relate to and coordinate with all of these kinds of people.

Even so, no one person has command of the vast arsenal of tools, helping skills and subspecialties of care that are available. My abilities are better suited for some depressed individuals than for others; certainly I am not able to help every melancholic person I encounter. All caregivers—whether they are full-time mental-health professionals or skilled generalists like parish clergy, nurses, and teachers—must always recognize and work within their limitations.

The best pastoral caregivers are willing to refer when needed, counsel, educate, challenge, or listen—and know when to do what. Mental-health professionals frequently refer their clients to others for specialized care when it is indicated; pastors should do no less for their parishioners. In fact, it is dubious ethically not to refer when an individual in your counsel needs the special expertise in a specific area of care. Referral is also indicated when a counselee's (or pastor's) prejudices or background make a trusting relationship difficult to achieve.

For ministers, referral is never total; it is not "dumping" the counselee. In one type of referral, pastoral caregivers surrender the major responsibility for care to another professional. This is imperative when depressed individuals are suicidal, psychotic, or severely depressed and in need of hospitalization. Unlike other helping professionals, however, pastors remain in the picture. They continue offering pastoral care to severely depressed parishioners, and remain their spiritual guides.

Also common in parish settings is a second type of referral, in which pastors are the primary caregivers for melancholics and their families but also send them to specialists for particular kinds of help. Referral to their primary-care physician for an examination should always be done in cases of major depression—even when it is mild—because there may be physical causes for the depressive symptoms or they may require antidepressant medications.

In medical referral, pastors take an active role. Remember the cognitive distortions of the depressed; they may not express their situation clearly to the physician and thus may not receive the care they need. It makes sense to teach counselees how to talk to their doctors. Help them form their statements: "I have heard four things in our conversation that your doctor should know about. Here's a pen so you can write them down." Once they have written a list complete with specific information about their depression as well as questions they need to ask, instruct them to bring the list along to the doctor's office. (If necessary, ask them to tell you how they will remember to take it.) A great many nondepressed individuals write down lists before seeing their physicians, but the depressed are unlikely to be so foresighted and clear-thinking.

Pastors also take an active role in finding and making referrals to community resources, such as financial advisers, attorneys, and employment counselors. They may consult with a depressed child's teacher or a food-service worker's employer. They work with counselees' family and friends. Even as primary caregivers, they refer.

Referral considers the counselee's mental and emotional states as well as the helper's limitations. Some depressed parishioners will resist seeing anyone other than their pastor and it may take some time to nudge them into going to a specialist. The minister's time, skill, and emotional objectivity also play a role in determining whether it is best to refer persons to more specialized care. When referral is needed, the following suggestions and resources may be of use.

Depression Awareness, Recognition, and Treatment (D/ART), National Institute of Mental Health (800) 421-4211
   www.nimh.nih.gov/publicat/index.htm

National Mental Health Association (800) 969-6642
   www.nmha.org/info/factsheets/index.html

American Association of Pastoral Counselors (AAPC) (703) 385-6967
   www.metanoia.org/aapc/

National Depressive and Manic-Depressive Association (800) 826-3632
   www.ndmda.org/

American Psychological Association
   www.apa.org

Healthguide Online Depression Information
   www.healthguide.com/dep

Know that depressed individuals will not always accept referral. Some will find that merely considering referral motivates them to change. Others may only want to complain about their situation and not work toward a resolution. Still others are so inactive and reclusive that talking to anyone (except the pastor) is more than they can tolerate.

When uncertain where to refer, call a mental-health professional in the congregation, a local crisis line, or an information and referral agency. Call one of the above listed national depression organizations. Explain the situation and get accurate information on the appropriate person or agency. A direct call to the agency will answer questions about waiting lists, fee schedules, and other pertinent information.

Suggest several referral sources, if possible, since one may be unavailable when it is needed.

Make concrete referrals—not "I think you need to see a psychotherapist" but "I'd be happy to recommend several marriage counselors; Dr. Fimbres was helpful for my neighbors, and Dr. Hetzel has a very good reputation."

If possible, let counselees make the referral call; suggest dialing the number immediately or offer a ride to the first appointment.

Except in an emergency, referral usually is *not* the first step in the care process. It is important to establish a relationship, listen carefully, and then gently move toward action, explaining carefully how the referral source can assist in the resolution. Some depressed individuals will tell pastors, "You are the only one who can help me" or "I wouldn't tell this to anyone but you" or even "I don't trust doctors (psychiatrists, therapists, marriage and family counselors)." Tell them that you appreciate their trust. "Now I need you to trust me when I tell you that you need to see Dr. Hetzel."

Always follow up after making a referral. For example, call counselees the next day to say "I called to find out how you are doing today and to see if you had any problems scheduling a session with Dr. Fimbres or Dr. Hetzel." If they answer with excuses, ask if there are other ways you can help, or if they want to see you for further discussion. Let them know that you will call again in a couple of days to see how they are doing. Neither harass people nor let them get off too easily.

Making referrals to outside professionals is not a sign of defeat; where indicated, it is the ethical thing to do, a mark of the pastor's insight and professionalism. For the depressed, it can be the first step in learning to manage depression.

Spiritual Import

If depression is increasing to levels never seen in recent memory, an anti-dote is urgently needed. That antidote, that food for the heart that hungers for God, is *hope* based upon God's grace. Pastoral caregivers listen carefully for the quiet murmurings of spirit within the words of those who are depressed. As they help suffering melancholics to make the cognitive, behavioral, interpersonal, and physiological changes necessary to emerge from their cavern, they do not forget those murmurings of spirit because they may also reflect the sufferings of one on the path of faith.

Spiritual suffering is akin to depression, and yet different in one criti-cal way: it is of ultimate significance because of its relationship to the Absolute. Ministers are uniquely equipped to offer assistance and hope not only for the clinically depressed but also for those whose journey of faith has led them to the arid desert, to the listless noonday demon, to darkness of spirit, to the cavern of despair.

The image and pain of my own bout with depression comes back to me from time to time. I can still see the cavern and feel the danger. It is impossible for me to forget the great impact of melancholia upon its suf-ferers and those around them, even when it is hidden. The depressed usu-ally do not draw a lot of attention to themselves; they are more likely to sit quietly in a corner and bother no one. Often their quiet despair goes unnoticed until it is more serious: they begin to perform poorly at work, isolate themselves from those around them, and even consider or attempt suicide. Understanding depression's effect upon cognition, physiology, interpersonal relationships, and behavior gives pastoral caregivers a clearer image of its various manifestations and disguises.

Pastoral care and counseling can help to lead the depressed out of the cavern, to reverse the downward spiral. As they shed some of their own pain, recovering melancholics are called in turn to assume some of the individual pain and global suffering of this world. Mature Christians achieve meaning through discipleship and a positive attitude toward life that relies on "the strength . . . through Him who gives me power" (Phil. 4:13 NEB). Ultimately, their true hope lies not only in the comfort and sup-port of others, but in God's redemptive grace and in their active response to God's call.

APPENDIX

The Zung Scale

Name: _____

Age: _____ Sex: _____ Date: _____

Instructions

Read each sentence carefully. For each statement, check the box in the column that best corresponds to how often you have felt that way during the past two weeks.

For statements 5 and 7, if you are on a diet, answer as if you were not.

	Please check a response for each of the 20 items	None or a little of the time	Some of the time	Good part of the time	Most or all of the time
1	I feel downhearted, blue, and sad	❏	❏	❏	❏
2	Morning is when I feel the best	❏	❏	❏	❏
3	I have crying spells or feel like it	❏	❏	❏	❏
4	I have trouble sleeping through the night	❏	❏	❏	❏
5	I eat as much as I used to	❏	❏	❏	❏
6	I enjoy looking at, talking to, and being with attractive women/men	❏	❏	❏	❏
7	I notice that I am losing weight	❏	❏	❏	❏
8	I have trouble with constipation	❏	❏	❏	❏
9	My heart beats faster than usual	❏	❏	❏	❏
10	I get tired for no reason	❏	❏	❏	❏
11	My mind is as clear as it used to be	❏	❏	❏	❏
12	I find it easy to do the things I used to do	❏	❏	❏	❏
13	I am restless and can't keep still	❏	❏	❏	❏
14	I feel hopeful about the future	❏	❏	❏	❏
15	I am more irritable than usual	❏	❏	❏	❏
16	I find it easy to make decisions	❏	❏	❏	❏
17	I feel that I am useful and needed	❏	❏	❏	❏
18	My life is pretty full	❏	❏	❏	❏
19	I feel that others would be better off if I were dead	❏	❏	❏	❏
20	I still enjoy the things I used to do	❏	❏	❏	❏

How to Use the Self-Rating Depression Scale

The Self-Rating Depression Scale (SDS) comprises a list of twenty items. Each item relates to a specific characteristic of depression. The twenty items together comprehensively delineate the symptoms of depression as they are widely recognized. Opposite the statements are four columns headed: *None or a little of the time, Some of the time, Good part of the time,* and *Most or all of the time.*

For each item on the form, the counselee is asked to check the box according to how it relates to his/her feelings within a specified time period: "during the past two weeks." Although some depressed counselees orally volunteer little information, most will readily cooperate when asked to check the scale if told that this will help the doctor know more about them.

The chart on the facing page will enable you to score the counselee's self-rating depression scale and find out the level of his or her depressive symptomatology.

Find the value of each of the twenty item responses by using the number next to the check mark. Total the scores to get the Raw Score. Next, use the conversion table (Raw Scores to SDS Index) at the bottom of the page and write the patient's SDS Index in the box at the bottom of the last column. The SDS Index is a total indication of "How depressed is the patient?" in terms of the operational definition and is expressed as a percentage. Thus, an SDS score of 65 may be interpreted to mean that the patient demonstrates 65% of the depression measurable by the scale.

By combining results from several studies, the SDS Index can be interpreted as follows:

SDS Index	Equivalent Clinical Global Impressions
Below 50	Within normal range, no psychopathology
50–59	Presence of minimal to mild depression
60–69	Presence of moderate to marked depression
70 and over	Presence of severe to extreme depression

These interpretations are based on data that compare depressed versus nondepressed patients as well as depressed patients versus normal subjects in the 20- to 64-year-old range. High scores are not in themselves diagnostic but indicate the presence of symptoms that may be of clinical significance.

Please check a response for each of the 20 items	None or a little of the time	Some of the time	Good part of the time	Most or all of the time
1 I feel downhearted, blue, and sad	❏ 1	❏ 2	❏ 3	❏ 4
2 Morning is when I feel the best	❏ 4	❏ 3	❏ 2	❏ 1
3 I have crying spells or feel like it	❏ 1	❏ 2	❏ 3	❏ 4
4 I have trouble sleeping through the night	❏ 1	❏ 2	❏ 3	❏ 4
5 I eat as much as I used to	❏ 4	❏ 3	❏ 2	❏ 1
6 I enjoy looking at, talking to, and being with attractive women/men	❏ 4	❏ 3	❏ 2	❏ 1
7 I notice that I am losing weight	❏ 1	❏ 2	❏ 3	❏ 4
8 I have trouble with constipation	❏ 1	❏ 2	❏ 3	❏ 4
9 My heart beats faster than usual	❏ 1	❏ 2	❏ 3	❏ 4
10 I get tired for no reason	❏ 1	❏ 2	❏ 3	❏ 4
11 My mind is as clear as it used to be	❏ 4	❏ 3	❏ 2	❏ 1
12 I find it easy to do the things I used to do	❏ 4	❏ 3	❏ 2	❏ 1
13 I am restless and can't keep still	❏ 1	❏ 2	❏ 3	❏ 4
14 I feel hopeful about the future	❏ 4	❏ 3	❏ 2	❏ 1
15 I am more irritable than usual	❏ 1	❏ 2	❏ 3	❏ 4
16 I find it easy to make decisions	❏ 4	❏ 3	❏ 2	❏ 1
17 I feel that I am useful and needed	❏ 4	❏ 3	❏ 2	❏ 1
18 My life is pretty full	❏ 4	❏ 3	❏ 2	❏ 1
19 I feel that others would be better off if I were dead	❏ 1	❏ 2	❏ 3	❏ 4
20 I still enjoy the things I used to do	❏ 4	❏ 3	❏ 2	❏ 1

Total (Raw Score) _____
SDS Index _____

Conversion of Raw Scores to SDS Index									
Raw Score	SDS Index	Raw Score	SDS Index	Raw Score	SDS Index	Raw Score	SDS Index	Raw Score	SDS Index
20	25	32	40	44	55	56	70	68	85
21	26	33	41	45	56	57	71	69	86
22	28	34	43	46	58	58	73	70	88
23	29	35	44	47	59	59	74	71	89
24	30	36	45	48	60	60	75	72	90
25	31	37	46	49	61	61	76	73	91
26	33	38	48	50	63	62	78	74	92
27	34	39	49	51	64	63	79	75	94
28	35	40	50	52	65	64	80	76	95
29	36	41	51	53	66	65	81	77	96
30	38	42	53	54	68	66	83	78	98
31	39	43	54	55	69	67	84	79	99
								80	100

Results from several studies have shown that there is usually some depressive symptomatology present in almost all of the psychiatric disorders. Patients may have several diagnoses: headache AND depression, schizophrenia AND depression, diabetes AND depression. Thus, a primary diagnosis other than depression does not eliminate the possibility that the patient is also depressed. If the SDS Index is above 50, the patient may need treatment for the depression in addition to treatment for the primary diagnosis.

Free copies of the Zung Self-Rating Scale are available to ministers. Contact:

Eli Lilly and Company
Lilly Corporate Center
U.S. Neuroscience, Constituency Relations
Drop Code 1047
Indianapolis, IN 46285
fax (317) 277-2387

Bibliography

Abplanap, J. M., A. F. Donnelly, & R. M. Rose. 1979. "Psychoendocrinology of the Menstrual Cycle: I. Enjoyment of Daily Activities and Moods." *Psychosomatic Medicine* 41:587–604.

American Psychiatric Association (APA). 1993. "Practice Guideline for Major Depressive Disorder in Adults." *American Journal of Psychiatry* 150:4, 1–26.

American Psychiatric Association (APA). 1994. *Diagnostic and Statistical Manual of Mental Disorders*, 4th ed., rev. Washington, D.C.: American Psychiatric Association.

Anderson, C., S. Dimidjian, & A. Miller. 1995. "Family Therapy." In I. D. Glick, ed. *Treating Depression*. San Francisco: Jossey-Bass, 1–32.

Andreasen, N. C. 1987. "Creativity and Mental Illness: Prevalence Rates in Writers and Their First-Degree Relatives." *American Journal of Psychiatry* 144:1288–92.

____, and I. D. Glick. 1988. "Bipolar Affective Disorder and Creativity: Implications and Clinical Management." *Comprehensive Psychiatry* 29:3, 207–17.

____, and A. Canter. 1974. "The Creative Writer: Psychiatric Symptoms and Family History." *Comprehensive Psychiatry* 15:123–31.

Antonuccio, D. O., W. G. Danton, and G. Y. DeNelsky. 1995. "Psychotherapy Versus Medication for Depression: Challenging the Conventional Wisdom with Data." *Professional Psychology: Research and Practice* 26:6, 574–85.

Assagioli, R. 1965. *Psychosythesis*. New York: Hobbs, Dorman & Company.

Bandler, R., and J. Grinder. 1979. *Frogs into Princes*. Moab, Utah: People Press.

Bateson, G. 1987. *Steps to an Ecology of Mind*. Northvale, N.J.: Jason Aronson.

Beach, S. R. H., and G. M. Nelson. 1990. "Pursuing Research on Major Psychopathology from a Contextual Perspective: The Example of Depression and Marital Discord." In G. Brody and I. E. Sigel, eds. *Family Research*. Vol. 2. Hillsdale, N.J.: Lawrence Erlbaum, 227–60.

____, E. E. Sandeen, and K. D. O'Leary. 1990. "A Randomized Clinical Trial of Inpatient Family Intervention: V. Results for Affective Disorders." *Journal of Affective Disorder* 18:17–28.

____. 1990a. *Depression in Marriage*. New York: Guilford.

Beck, A. T. 1967. *Depression*. New York: Harper and Row.

____. 1976. *Cognitive Therapy and the Emotional Disorders*. New York: International Universities Press.

____. 1991. "Cognitive Therapy: A 30-Year Retrospective." *American Psychologist* 46:4, 368–75.

____, G. Brown, R. A. Steer, J. I. Eidelson, and J. H. Riskind. 1979. *Cognitive Therapy of Depression.* New York: Guilford.

Benner, A. E. 1992. *Strategic Pastoral Counseling: A Short-Term Structure Model.* Grand Rapids: Baker.

Berg, I. K., and S. D. Miller. 1992. *Working with the Problem Drinker: A Solution-Focused Approach.* New York: W. W. Norton.

Bernard, J. 1972. *The Future of Marriage.* New York: World.

Billings, A. G., and R. H. Moos. 1982. "Psychosocial Theory and Research in Depression: An Integrative Framework and Review." *Clinical Psychology Review* 2: 213–38.

Bloom, B., S. J. Asher, and S. W. White. 1978. "Marital Disruption as a Stressor: A Review and Analysis." *Psychological Bulletin* 85:867–94.

Bloomfield, M. 1952. *Seven Deadly Sins.* East Lansing: Michigan State College Press.

Breggin, P., and G. R. Breggin. 1994. *Talking Back to Prozac.* New York: St. Martin's.

Bringle, M. L. 1990. *Despair: Sickness or Sin? Hopelessness and Healing in the Christian Life.* Nashville: Abingdon.

____. 1996. "Soul-Dye and Salt: Integrating Spiritual and Medical Understandings of Depression." *Journal of Pastoral Care* 40:329–40.

Brown, G. W., and T. O. Harris. 1978. *Social Origins of Depression: A Study of Psychiatric Disorder in Women.* New York: Free Press.

Burns, D. 1980. *Feeling Good: New Mood Therapy.* New York: Morrow.

Capps, D. 1993. *The Depleted Self.* Minneapolis: Fortress.

Casey, M. 1995. *Sacred Reading.* Liguori, Mo.: Triumph Books

Chafetz, J. S. 1979. *Masculine, Feminine or Human?* Itasca, Ill.: Peacock.

Cleve, Jay. 1989. *Out of the Blue.* Minneapolis: CompCare.

Clinebell, H. 1984. *Basic Types of Pastoral Care and Counseling.* Nashville: Abingdon.

Cowley, G. 1994. "The Culture of Prozac." *Newsweek* (7 February):41–42.

Coyne, J. C. 1986. "Strategic Marital Therapy for Depression." In N. S. Jacobson and A. S. Gurman, eds. *Clinical Handbook of Marital Therapy.* New York: Guilford. 495–511.

Damasio, A. 1997. "Towards a Neuropathology of Emotion and Mood." *Nature* 386 (24 April):769–70.

Daw, J. 1995. "Alcohol Abuse and Depression." *Family Therapy News* 26 (16 October):5.

Dayringer, R. 1995. *Dealing with Depression.* New York: Haworth.

de Shazer, S. 1985. *Keys to Solution in Brief Therapy.* New York: W. W. Norton.

____. 1988. *Clues: Investigating Solutions in Brief Therapy.* New York: W. W. Norton.

____. 1991. *Putting Difference to Work.* New York: W. W. Norton.

DeBattista, C., and A. Schatzberg. 1995. "Somatic Therapy." In I. Glick, ed. *Treating Depression.* San Francisco: Jossey-Bass, 153–81.

DeRosis, H., and V. Pellegrina. 1976. *The Book of Hope*. New York: McMillan.

Elkin, I., T. M. Shea, J. T. Watkins, S. D. Imber, S. M. Sotsky, J. F. Collins, D. R. Glass, P. A. Pilkonis, W. R. Leber, J. P. Docherty, S. J. Fiester, and M. B. Parloff. 1989. "NIMH Treatment of Depression Collaborative Research Program." *Archives of General Psychiatry* 46:971–82.

Elkin, I. 1994. "The NIMH Treatment of Depression Collaborative Research Program: Where We Began and Where We Are." In S. L. Garfield and A. E. Bergin *Handbook of Psychotherapy and Behavior Change*. 4th ed. New York: Wiley. 114–39.

Evagrius of Pontus. 1970. *The Praktikos*. Edited and translated by J. Bamberger. Spencer, Mass.: Cistercian Publications.

Fairchild, R. W. 1980. *Finding Hope Again: A Pastor's Guide to Counseling Depressed Persons*. New York: Harper and Row.

Farberow, N., S. Heilig, and R. Litman. 1968. *Techniques in Crisis Intervention: A Training Manual*. Los Angeles: Suicide Prevention Center, Inc.

Fawcett, J. 1993. "The Morbidity and Mortality of Clinical Depression." *International Clinical Psychopharmacology* 8:217–20.

Ferdon, J. 1983. *How the Contemplative Approach to Spiritual Direction Aids Women Religious in Dealing with Depression*. Weston School of Theology Ph.D. dissertation.

Field, T., B. Healy, S. Goldstein, and M. Guthertz. 1990. "Behavior-State Matching and Synchrony in Mother-Infant Interactions of Nondepressed Versus Depressed Dyads." *Developmental Psychology* 26:7–14.

Frankl, V. 1963. *Man's Search for Meaning*. New York: Washington Square Press.

Frost, Christopher J. 1985. *Religious Melancholy or Psychological Depression?* Boston: University Press of America.

Gaddy, C. W. 1991. *A Soul under Siege*. Louisville: Westminster John Knox.

Ganss, G., ed. 1991. *Ignatius of Loyola: The Spiritual Exercises and Selected Works*. Mahwah, N.J.: Paulist.

Goffman, E. 1974. *Frame Analysis*. Rockville: Aspen.

Gold, M. 1986. *The Good News about Depression*. New York: Bantam.

Gordon, D., D. Burge, C. Hammen, C. Adrian, C. Jaenicke, and D. Hiroto. 1989. "Observations of Interactions of Depressed Women with Their Children." *American Journal of Psychiatry* 146:50–55.

Gove, W. R., M. Hughes, and C. B. Style. 1983. "Does Marriage Have Positive Effects on the Psychological Well-Being of an Individual?" *Journal of Health and Social Behavior* 24:122–31.

Greg-Schroeder, S. 1997. *In the Shadow of God's Wings*. Nashville: Upper Room.

Gregory the Great. 1950. *Pastoral Care*. Translated by H. Davis. Westminster, Md.: Newman.

Gritsch, E. 1983. *Martin—God's Court Jester: Luther in Retrospective.* Philadelphia: Fortress.

____, and R. Jenson. 1976. *Lutheranism: The Theological Movement and Its Confessional Writings.* Philadelphia: Fortress.

Haley, J. 1973. *Uncommon Therapy: The Psychiatric Techniques of Milton H. Erickson, M.D.* New York: W. W. Norton.

____. 1984. *Ordeal Therapy.* San Francisco: Jossey-Bass.

Hamilton, M. 1969. "A Rating Scale for Depression." *Journal of Neurology, Neurosurgery, and Psychiatry* 23:56–62.

Hammen, C., D. Burge, E. Burney, and C. Adrian. 1990. "Longitudinal Study of Diagnoses in Children of Women with Unipolar and Bipolar Affective Disorder. *Archives of General Psychiatry* 47:1112–17.

Hart, A. D. 1984. *Coping with Depression in the Ministry and Other Helping Professions.* Waco: Word.

Hassler, J. 1985. *A Green Journey.* New York: Ballantine.

Hauck, P. 1976. *Overcoming Depression.* Philadelphia: Westminster.

Hohmann, A. A., and D. B. Larson. 1993. "Psychiatric Factors Predicting Use of Clergy." In *Psychotherapy and Religious Values.* Edited by E. L. Worthington Jr. Grand Rapids: Baker. 71–84.

Hollon, S., R. DeRubeis, and M. Seligman. 1992. "Cognitive Therapy and the Prevention of Depression." *Applied and Preventive Psychology* 1:89–95.

Hulme, W. and L. Hulme. 1995. *Wrestling with Depression.* Minneapolis: Augsburg.

Ilfeld, F. W. 1977. "Current Social Stressors and Symptoms of Depression." *American Journal of Psychiatry* 134:161–66.

Jackson, P. B. 1992. "Specifying the Buffering Hypothesis: Support, Strain, and Depression." *Social Psychology Quarterly* 55(4):363–78.

Jacobson, N. S. 1992. "Behavioral Couple Therapy: A New Beginning." *Behavior Therapy* 25:452–62.

____, K. Dobson, A. E. Fruzzetti, D. B. Schmaling, and S. Salusky. 1991. "Marital Therapy as a Treatment for Depression." *Journal of Consulting and Clinical Psychology* 59:547–57.

Jarrett, R., and J. Rush. 1994. "Short-Term Psychotherapy of Depressive Disorders: Current Status and Future Direction." *Psychiatry* 57:2, 115–32.

Jordan, M. 1986. *Taking on the Gods.* Nashville: Abingdon.

Juda, A. 1949. "The Relationship between Highest Mental Capacity and Psychic Abnormalities." *American Journal of Psychiatry* 106:296–307.

Kavanaugh, A. 1987. *The Dark Night of the Soul in St. John of the Cross: Selected Writings,* Classics of Western Spirituality. Mahwah, N.J.: Paulist.

Kazdin, A. E. 1989. "Childhoo ' Depression." In E. J. Mash and R. A. Barkley, eds. *Treatment of Childhood Disorders.* New York: Guilford, 495–511.

Keitner, G. I., I. W. Miller, N. B. Epstein, and D. S. Bishop. 1986. "The Functioning in Families of Patients with Major Depression." *International Journal of Family Psychiatry* 7:11–16.

Kessler, R. C., and M. Essex. 1982. "Marital Status and Depression: The Importance of Coping Resources." *Social Forces* 61:484–507.

Kierkegaard, S. 1954. *Fear and Trembling/The Sickness unto Death*. Translated by W. Lowrie. Garden City, N.Y.: Doubleday Anchor.

Kramer, P. 1993. *Listening to Prozac*. New York: Viking.

Larson, D. B., A. A. Hohmann, L. G. Kessler, and K. G. Meador. 1988. "The Couch and the Cloth: The Need for Linkage." *Hospital and Community Psychiatry* 39:1064–69.

Lazarus, A. 1972. *Behavior Therapy and Beyond*. New York: McGraw-Hill.

Lester, A. 1995. *Hope in Pastoral Care and Counseling*. Westminster/John Knox.

Lewinsohn, P. M., R. F. Munoz, M. A. Youngren, and A. M. Zeiss. 1978. *Control Your Depression*. Englewood Cliffs, N.J.: Prentice-Hall.

Lieberman, R. P. 1981. "A Model for Individualizing Treatment." In L. Rehm, ed. *Behavioral Therapy for Depression*. New York: Academic.

Loftus, J. A. 1983. *Some Relationships between Spiritual Desolation as Defined in the First Week of the Spiritual Exercises of Ignatius Loyola and Clinical Depression as Presented in Contemporary Psychological Theories*. Boston University Graduate School Ph.D. dissertation.

Luibheid, C., trans. 1985. *John Cassian: Conferences*. Classics of Western Spirituality. Mahwah, N.J.: Paulist.

Luther, M. 1955. *Letters of Spiritual Counsel*. Edited and translated by T. Tappert. Philadelphia: Westminster Press.

Lutheran Book of Worship. 1978. Minneapolis: Augsburg.

Madanes, C. 1984. *Behind the One-Way Mirror*. San Francisco: Jossey-Bass.

McGrath, E., G. Keita, B. Strickland, and N. Russo, eds. 1990. *Women and Depression: Risk Factors and Treatment Issues*. Washington, D.C.: American Psychological Association.

Meadow, M. J. 1984. "The Dark Side of Mysticism: Depression and 'The Dark Night.'" *Pastoral Psychology* 33:2, 105–125.

Meltzer, H. 1990. "Role of Serotonin in Depression." *Annals New York Academy of Sciences* 325:9, 486–500.

Munoz, R. F., Y. Ying, E. Perez-Stable and J. Miranda. 1993. *The Prevention of Depression*. Baltimore: Johns Hopkins University Press.

Neuger, C. C. 1991. "Women's Depression: Lives at Risk." In M. Glaz and J. S. Moessner, eds. *Women in Travail and Transition*. Minneapolis: Fortress, 146–61.

O'Hanlon, W. H., and M. Weiner-Davis. 1989. *In Search of Solutions*. New York: W. W. Norton.

Palmer, P. 1995. "Action and Insight: An Interview with Parker Palmer." *The Christian Century* (22–29 March):326–29.

Pollock, E. 1995. "Managed Care's Focus on Psychiatric Drugs Alarms Many Doctors." *Wall Street Journal* xcvi:107 (1 December):A1, A4.

Potter, W., M. Rudorfer, and H. Manji. 1991. "The Pharmacologic Treatment of Depression." *New England Journal of Medicine* 325:9 (29 August):633–42.

Prien, R. F., D. J. Kupfer, P. A. Mansky, J. G. Small, V. B. Twason, C. G. Voss, and W. E. Johnson. 1984. "Drug Therapy in the Prevention of Recurrences in Unipolar and Bipolar Affective Disorders: Report of the NIMH Collaborative Study Group Comparing Lithium Carbonate, Imipramine, and a Lithium Carbonate–Imipramine Combination." *Archives of General Psychiatry* 41:1096–1104.

Prince, S., and N. Jacobson. 1995. "A Review and Evaluation of Marital and Family Therapies for Affective Disorders." *Journal of Marital and Family Therapy* 21:377–401.

Propst, L., et al. 1992. "Comparative Efficacy of Religious and Nonreligious Cognitive-Behavioral Therapy for the Treatment of Clinical Depression in Religious Individuals." *Journal of Consulting and Clinical Psychology* 60:94–103.

Radke-Yarrow, M., E. Nottlemann, B. Belmont, and J. D. Welsh. 1993. "Affective Interactions of Depressed and Nondepressed Mothers." *Journal of Abnormal Child Psychology* 21:683–95.

Raskin, A., et al. 1970. "Differential Response to Chlorpromazine, Imipramine, and Placebo: A Study of Sub-Groups of Hospitalized Depressed Patients." *Archives of General Psychiatry* 23:163–73.

Regier, D., et al. 1993. "The de facto U.S. Mental Health and Addictive Disorders Service System." *Archives of General Psychiatry* 50:85–94.

Rossi, E., M. Ryan, and F. Sharp. 1983. *Healing in Hypnosis: The Seminars, Workshops, and Lectures of Milton H. Erickson.* Vol. 1. New York: Irvington.

Roy, A. 1978. "Vulnerability Factors and Depression in Women." *British Journal of Psychiatry* 133:106–10.

_____. 1987. "Five Risk Factors for Depression." *British Journal of Psychiatry* 150:536–41.

Rupp, G., 1953. *The Righteousness of God.* London: Hodder and Stoughton.

Seligman, M. 1973. "Fall into Helplessness." *Psychology Today* 7:43–48.

_____. 1974. "Depression and Learned Helplessness." In R. Friedman and M. Katz, eds. *The Psychology of Depression: Contemporary Theory and Research.* Washington, D.C.: Winston, 144–61.

_____. 1975. *Helplessness: On Depression, Development, and Health.* San Francisco: Freeman.

_____. 1983. "Learned Helplessness." In *Depression: Concepts, Controversies, and Some New Facts.* 2nd ed. Hillsdale, N.J.: Erlbaum, 64–72.

_____. 1990. *Learned Optimism.* New York: Alfred A. Knopf.

_____. 1990a. "Why Is There So Much Depression Today? The Waxing of the Individual and the Waning of the Commons." In R. Ingram, ed.

Contemporary Psychological Approaches to Depression: Theory, Research, and Treatment. New York: Plenum.

Snyder, S. 1965. "The Left Hand of God: Despair in Medieval and Renaissance Tradition." *Studies in the Renaissance* 12:59.

Sotsky, S., D. R. Glass, M. T. Shea, P. A. Pilkonis, J. F. Collins, I. Elkin, J. T. Watkins, S. D. Imber, W. R. Leber, J. Moyer, and M. E. Oliveri. 1991. "Patient Prediction of Response to Psychotherapy and Pharmacotherapy: Findings in the NIMH Treatment of Depression Collaborative Research Program." *American Journal of Psychiatry* 148:8, 997–1008.

Stone, H. W. 1972. *Suicide and Grief.* Philadelphia: Fortress.

_____. 1980. *Using Behavioral Methods in Pastoral Counseling.* Philadelphia: Fortress.

_____. 1996. *Theological Context for Pastoral Caregiving.* New York: Haworth.

_____. 1991. *The Caring Church: A Guide for Lay Pastoral Care.* 2nd ed., rev. Minneapolis: Fortress.

_____. 1993. *Crisis Counseling.* 2nd ed., rev. Minneapolis: Fortress.

_____. 1994. *Brief Pastoral Counseling.* Minneapolis: Fortress.

_____, and W. Clements. 1991. *Handbook for Basic Types of Pastoral Care and Counseling.* Nashville: Abingdon.

_____, and J. Duke. 1996. *How to Think Theologically.* Minneapolis: Fortress.

Tellenbach, H. 1980. *Melancholy.* Pittsburgh: Duquesne University Press.

U.S. Department of Health and Human Services. 1993. *Detection and Diagnosis.* Vol. 1 of *Depression in Primary Care.* Clinical Practice Guideline, no. 5.

_____. 1993. *Treatment of Major Depression.* Vol. 2 of *Depression in Primary Care.* Clinical Practice Guideline, no. 5.

Uhlenhuth, E. H., M. D. Baltes, R. S. Lipman, and S. J. Haberman. 1977. "Remembering Life Events." In J. Strauss, H. Babigian, and M. Roff, eds. *The Origins and Course of Psychopathology.* New York: Plenum.

Underhill, E. 1955. *Mysticism: A Study in the Nature and Development of Man's Spiritual Consciousness.* New York: Meridian.

Walter, J. and J. Peller. 1992. *Becoming Solution-Focused in Brief Therapy.* New York: Brunner/Mazel.

Watzlawick, P., J. H. Weakland, and R. Fisch. 1974. *Change: Principles of Problem Formation and Problem Resolution.* New York: W. W. Norton.

Weiner-Davis, M., S. de Shazer, and W. J. Gingerich. 1987. "Building on Pretreatment Changes to Construct the Therapeutic Solution: An Exploratory Study." *Journal of Marital and Family Therapy* 13 (4):359–63.

Weissman, M. M. 1987. "Advances in Psychiatric Epidemiology: Rates and Risks for Major Depression." *American Journal of Public Health* 77:445–51.

_____, and G. L. Klerman. 1985. "Sex Differences in the Epidemiology of Depression." *Archives of General Psychiatry* 34:98–111.

Wells, R. 1982. *Planned Short-Term Treatment.* New York: Free Press.

Wenzel, S. 1967. *The Sin of Sloth: Acedia in Medieval Thought and Literature.* Chapel Hill, N.C.: University of North Carolina Press.

White, M. 1987. "Family Therapy and Schizophrenia: Addressing the 'In-The-Corner' Lifestyle." *Dulwich Centre Newsletter* Spring:14–21.

————. 1989. *Selected Papers.* Adelaide, Australia: Dulwich Centre Publications.

Yapko, M. D. 1989. *Behavioral Approach to Treating Anxiety and Depression.* New York: Brunner/Mazel.

————, ed. 1986. *Hypnotic and Strategic Intervention: Principles and Practice.* New York: Irvington.

————. 1994. *When Living Hurts: Directives for Treating Depression.* New York: Brunner/Mazel.

————. 14 September 1996 speech. "Listening to Prozac . . . But Talking to Clients: Brief Methods for Treating Depression," Our Lady of the Lake, University of San Antonio.

Zung, W. W. 1965. "A Self-Rating Depression Scale." *Archives of General Psychiatry* 23:63–70.

Index

About the Author

Howard W. Stone is internationally renowned in the field of pastoral care and counseling for his many contributions to the understanding and practice of professional and lay ministry. His practical and effective books have been widely influential and translated into a half-dozen languages. Professor of Psychology and Pastoral Counseling at Brite Divinity School, Texas Christian University, Fort Worth, Texas, Stone is also editor of the Fortress Press series Creative Pastoral Care and Counseling and a frequent lecturer and workshop leader.